LOUIS B. WRIGHT · THEODORE HORNBERGER

ROBERT E. SPILLER · STANLEY T. WILLIAMS

HENRY NASH SMITH · LEON HOWARD

The American Writer
and the European Tradition

WILLARD THORP · CLARENCE GOHDES

ALFRED KAZIN · LIONEL TRILLING

NORMAN HOLMES PEARSON · HARRY LEVIN

Margaret Denny and William H. Gilman
editors

PUBLISHED FOR THE University of Rochester BY
THE UNIVERSITY OF MINNESOTA PRESS, Minneapolis

Copyright 1950 by the
UNIVERSITY OF MINNESOTA

PRINTED AT THE COLWELL PRESS, INC., MINNEAPOLIS

London, Geoffrey Cumberlege, Oxford University Press

Editors' Foreword

THE twelve essays of this volume were originally delivered as lectures in a series of four conferences at the University of Rochester in the winter of 1948–49. The theme of the conferences—the American writer and the European tradition—was chosen because of its crucial importance today. America seems called upon to produce a literature which will nourish and refresh European readers; at the same time it needs to perceive more clearly the source and nature of formative influences, both past and present, upon its literature. We need to know to what degree and for what reasons a European feels a shock of recognition when he reads an American work; we need to find better means of evaluating what the European reader may consider untraditional and "native."

Does the excellence of American writers of undisputed merit rest to an appreciable degree upon their debt to or their independence of the European tradition? Do American writers tend to restate European concepts or are they more prone to reinterpret them? What happens when American writers turn their backs on Europe? What is it that makes an American author peculiarly American? Without a studied search for the answers, we can be as baffled as Huck Finn was by Jim's notorious *petitio principii*. We can be reduced to saying that an American writer is American because he writes like an American. And without deeper study of our debts to Europe and of our impact abroad, we are in danger of ignoring the whole progress of our times toward the acknowledgment that we live in one world.

The essays in this volume bear upon some aspect of the questions raised above. Individually they make notable contributions of fresh points of view and cogent statements; they set familiar facts in new patterns. In style and spirit the essays are informal. The signal success of the conferences at which they were delivered tends to justify the belief that even a complex and insufficiently explored subject may well be approached through criticism that is unpretentious in tone and offered in a spirit of inquiry rather than of pronouncement. In the audience at Rochester were freshmen and graduate students, guests from the community and college professors. Whatever their intellectual degree, their response was warm and their queries in the discussion periods bore witness to the stimulation of the lectures. There is reason to believe, therefore, that this volume will prove as interesting and profitable to the general reader as to the scholar.

The order of the essays in this volume, which corresponds to the sequence of their presentation at Rochester, is both chronological and topical. The subject matter of the first three moves from the English Renaissance through the Enlightenment to the union of the colonial and cosmopolitan minds in Franklin. The next four study the intellectual dispositions and behavior of American writers from Irving to Henry James, not in the conventional literary role of romanticists and realists, but as children of two cultural parents. The last group of essays opens with a study of the surprising impact on the maternal culture of its nineteenth-century children. Then three essays bring down to our times the intellectual biography of the American novelist and the poet under the stimulus of both inheritance and environment. The volume closes with a study of the altered roles of cultural parent and offspring.

Both the continuity and the topical unity of the papers arose from basic questions posed by the editors. These were, in effect: What was the original heritage of European ideas in America, and how have European ideas continued to influence American men of letters?
What ideas, what ways of thinking, and what intellectual attitudes are indigenous to America?

What, in outline, have been the reception and the influence of American letters in Europe?

The editors also suggested the original topics for the essays, though at all times they have rigorously shunned the part of Procrustes. Each author shaped his paper to the three major questions as he saw fit. A few took the opportunity to read their predecessors' papers before composing their own; most of them worked independently. Despite the diversity of preparation, the essays, taken collectively, yield some patterns of American intellectual and esthetic history which may be fairly well defined.

One major motif is the force and the persistence in America of European ideas and intellectual habits, or of the idea of Europe itself. At the outset Dr. Wright selects the code of the Renaissance gentleman to illustrate the formidable power of European ideals in shaping early American conduct. From Richard Lee to Thomas Jefferson, he locates the major impulse for men's actions in the ancient concepts of virtue and of service to the state. Thus the habit of looking to Europe for inspiration, of thinking in the European manner, Dr. Wright implies, became the core of the American heritage.

The inseparability of the European way and the American way is clear in Professor Hornberger's study of the Enlightenment and the American Dream. The ideas of equality, of distributed powers of government, and of social planning have such mixed origins that it is impossible to determine an exact national genealogy. And even if an indigenously American way of thought emerges in Franklin, as Professor Spiller finds, yet he perpetuated the Old World belief in the cultivation of virtue, he was thoroughly familiar with European theory, and he gave over the afternoon of his life to a successful pursuit of cosmopolitan breadth.

The enormous influence of European ideas, especially as embodied in literature, art, and manners, is inescapably clear in Professor Williams' study of cosmopolitanism in nineteenth-century America. The sense of exile from the cultural home to which the transplanted men of the Renaissance and even the men of the Enlightenment had felt reassuringly close echoes and re-echoes in the pages of Irving, Longfellow, James, and others. European scenes, European books, the European mind—these were of profound importance to writers and the public alike a hundred years ago, and Professor Williams finds a variety of explanations for the phenomenon. Even in such an apparent nativist as Mark Twain, Professor Smith shows, some of the cultural ideals of European liberals were a potent if perhaps unacknowledged force. Old concepts of the superiority of nature over civilization and of the Noble Savage are ironically reflected in writings which seem to flow from purely native springs.

The power of European philosophy, literature, and tradition in supplying energy for American literary men is the point of departure for Professor Howard's provocative analysis of Emerson, Hawthorne, Melville, and others. And in the American writer's conduct in political or social crises, which Professor Thorp studies, one may discern a European dedication to ideas. For Professor Trilling, the European capacity for the mature exercise of the intellect, or for the infusion of art with ideas, is the quality which marks the successful American prose writer today; and he is happy to find the poets in command of the tradition. Finally, the continuing impact of Europe is implicit in Professor Pearson's survey of modern American poets in relation to science, for many of the ideas which they both assimilate and transcend are foreign in origin.

The second question proposed for the conferences—what can be called indigenously American?—has produced some notable replies; for besides offering definitions the authors have also evaluated the artistic results of resisting or ignoring Europe. Thanks to their ordered arguments, their suggestions, or the inferences that may be drawn from their remarks, we can come to a clearer understanding of the term *American*. Thus Professor Spiller's essay on Franklin perceives an essential American quality in his habit of modifying European thought to accord with American circumstances.

Professor Howard skillfully develops a similar concept to explain six major writers who seem both indisputably in the European tradition and at the same time unmistakably American. Their tendency to transform European literary or philosophical tradition into something that makes sense in terms of their personal experience Professor Howard calls their "distinctive American characteristic." The varied effects of turning the back upon this European tradition appear in Professor Smith's inquiry into the origins of the native tradition. There are the excellencies of expression and effect that come when such a writer as Mark Twain works outside the heritage of English style; there is the glorification of the vernacular, with its democratic implications; but there are also defective taste, and intellectual naiveté, and the failure to develop a formal structure.

Mr. Kazin's paper needs to be read in the light of Professor Spiller's and Professor Howard's. His remarks on Dreiser imply that Dreiser could express deterministic ideas with power and conviction because determinism did not remain for him a mere European theory but was a pattern in observed life which confirmed the theory. And Professor Trilling's paper has links with Professor Smith's, for he also sees the breakdown in the American artist who fails to treat ideas dynamically.

What Professor Trilling has to say about the failure of contemporary writers to deal cogently with the traditional ideas of American social and political philosophy needs to be compared with the essay by Professor Thorp on American writers as critics of nineteenth-century society. Professor Thorp believes that because Emerson, Thoreau, Whitman, and Melville both thought and lived democratically, because "they were realists in their social thinking," they spoke effectively and took positive action in crises. What caused Mark Twain, Professor Thorp suggests, to turn into a "sour liberal," to repudiate the American tradition with much the same violence he visited on the European tradition, was his failure to analyze the abstract principles which energized his own life and his finest works. The intellectual collapse of Mark Twain, who is popularly considered the most "American" of our writers, as well as the failure of contemporary writers discussed by Professor Trilling, suggests the hypothesis that the American writer who cuts himself off from the European habit of abstract thinking is courting disaster.

American writers have thus been at times imitators, assimilators, and antagonists of European ideas and the European tradition. What, now, of their European reception? In what role did Europe applaud them most? Professors Gohdes and Levin give us some answers. The first makes it clear that though Longfellow was perhaps the most popular poet in the world, such writers as Cooper, Bret Harte, Mark Twain, and the western humorists were as well received as Irving, Emerson, and Poe. It would seem, then, that the American writer's popularity abroad had little to do with his intellectual relation to the European tradition. Europe seemed cordial, on the whole, not only to the writer whose manner scarcely differed from that of its own poets and essayists, but also to the distinctly native American. With some exceptions, it is still so disposed in the twentieth century, as Professor Levin shows us. He pictures our cultural penetration of England and the Continent and the mixed submission and resistance, the strange phenomenon of European imitations of American writers, and the acumen and astigmatism among European critics. He leaves us to lament the inability of America to assume a cultural leadership proportionate to its practical accomplishment; but he leaves us cause for hope in the habit of self-criticism and in our power to cultivate the fertile ground that lies somewhere between our native Americanism and the European tradition.

What generalizations are to be drawn from these essays as a whole? That common conclusions rise from the series is impressive proof of the essays' underlying unity and the dynamic relation they bear to each other. Thus Professor Levin's feeling that America's literary salvation lies somewhere between the work of the "pioneer" and that of the "expatriate" is a kind of formula to which most of the essays contribute symbols. Other general implications from these exploratory essays may be advanced at least as hypotheses.

It seems that if American scholars are to make full critical judgments of an American writer, they must always consider the extent to which the European tradition influenced him. The American writer cannot be considered as merely a cosmopolitan or a nativist. The American writer's success can best be tested by his capacity for either naturalizing an imported idea or charging his created product with the force of ideas. We can expect some kind of action, some practice of putting ideas to work, to mark the distinguished American writer. And we can expect an extension of commendable American influences abroad if the American writer, discarding the mere violence which is now his forte but not the natural virtue which is his real strength, reunites himself with the best of the European tradition.

MARGARET DENNY
WILLIAM H. GILMAN

May 1950

Table of Contents

*The American Writer
and the European Tradition*

⤳ LOUIS B. WRIGHT ⤳

The Renaissance Tradition in America

AMERICANS need, as never before, to know more about their origins and history. Suddenly we as a nation have been thrust into a position of leadership in the world. The future salvation of civilization literally depends upon our wisdom. And the development of our wisdom requires that we comprehend more intelligently the development of our own civilization, particularly in its relations to other civilizations. We urgently need to acquire historical perspective. There is no more fatal heresy than the glib assertion, too often made by certain dogmatists, that history has nothing beneficial to teach us.

We Americans have inherited a great tradition from the past, a tradition which has had a tremendous influence on the kinds of men and women we are today. Unhappily we are often ignorant of that tradition. Too often we dismiss the history of earlier periods as of no importance to Americans today.

As a result of the patriotic fervor stirred by the war, we have had a demand from school boards, politicians, patrioteers, and others for more courses in American history in high schools and colleges. For instance, in California, by decree of the legislature, every college student must show that he has had a course in American history or must pass a satisfactory examination therein before he is permitted to graduate.

Many legislators and patriots seem to believe that we can insure our social salvation with one required course in American history—any course. Now we all know what happens when a course is required, particularly by act of the legislature. Legislators and superpatriots also have a naive faith in required

3

courses in something called "Americanism"—whatever that is. They seem to think that there is a body of accepted historical dogma which can be memorized, and that the act of repeating the texts will somehow make good citizens. Such courses are about as effective as Tibetan prayer wheels.

But we do need good history—good American history—American history which begins a long way back with a thrilling and moving story of the beginnings of our modern civilization in the period which, for want of a better term, we call the Renaissance. For Americans, as no other people, are the inheritors of a body of ideas, a body of ideals, and patterns of behavior which have ancient antecedents. What happened in sixteenth- and seventeenth-century Europe, particularly England, was profoundly influential upon a nation yet to be born.

Historians worry a great deal about the definition of the word *Renaissance,* about its connotations and varied meanings. For the purposes of this discussion, I want to use *Renaissance* merely as a term of convenience to mean the social, spiritual, and intellectual upheaval which transformed and modernized Europe in the sixteenth and seventeenth centuries.

We may not realize it, but the Renaissance had much in common with our own age. Both periods saw epochal intellectual and social revolutions. Both periods saw earth-shaking developments in science. Both periods saw the horizons of the universe expanded with explosive repercussions. Both periods emphasized the power of the human mind, sometimes with egotistic arrogance.

Dr. Faustus, contemplating the power of his infinite knowledge, gained from the barter of his soul to the devil, could boast:

> All things that move between the quiet poles
> Shall be at my command. . . .
> Shall I make spirits fetch me what I please,
> Resolve me of all ambiguities
> Perform what desperate enterprise I will?
> I'll have them fly to India for gold
> Ransack the ocean for orient pearl
> And search all corners of the new-found world . . .

4

Yea, stranger engines for the brunt of war
Than was the fiery keel at Antwerp's bridge,
I'll make my servile spirits to invent.[1]

Faustus has returned in the twentieth century, and he presides over the uranium piles at Chicago, Hanford, and Oak Ridge. Once more his minions are searching all corners of the new-found world and inventing strange engines of war.

It is not this aspect of the Renaissance that I want to discuss, however, but rather the qualities of training and leadership which the Renaissance bequeathed us, qualities we need today more acutely than we have ever needed them.

The men and women who came to this country from 1607 onward brought with them a stock of inherited ideas which took fresh root in the New World and in many cases flourished with renewed vigor. Although we must remember that the majority of the settlers were not men of letters and learning, a saving remnant of leaders in both the southern colonies and New England had a sound classical education of the traditional sort provided by the grammar schools and universities. The leaders, as well as many humbler folk, were determined that the children of the new settlers should not "grow up barbarous in the wilderness"— to use a phrase which constantly recurs in the letters and writings of colonial America. It is significant that colonial Americans were desperately eager to reproduce the best of the older civilization which they had left. Indeed, this conservation of culture is one of the most important facts in the moving frontier, from Jamestown in 1607 to San Francisco in 1849. The first permanent structure erected at Jamestown, a church, also served as a school; and the first parson brought along a chest of books, which he used as a lending library. One of the first settlers, a university man named George Sandys, improved his few idle moments by translating Ovid's *Metamorphoses*. Captain John Smith, not usually remembered as a man of gentle manners, ordered the men of a wood-chopping squad to stop swearing over the pain to their blistered hands. For every oath, the swearer was to have one can of ice-cold water poured down his sleeve!

5

The American Writer and the European Tradition

Few of us today realize how much we owe to the efforts of hard-working colonists of the seventeenth and early eighteenth centuries in establishing and maintaining a civilized society. Even fewer of us realize the tremendous social contributions of the landed aristocracy which established itself in the same period. It has not been fashionable to say a good word for aristocracy in our times. We are inclined to equate aristocracy with the decadent French aristocracy of the period of Louis XVI, or the equally decadent Russian aristocracy of 1916–17. We forget that most of our own traditional liberties were won by substantial country gentlemen in collaboration with equally substantial members of the rising middle class who themselves aspired to be gentlemen.

One of the most important ideas brought to America in the intellectual luggage of these seventeenth-century settlers was the concept of the Renaissance gentleman, the type of gentleman developed in England during the reigns of Elizabeth and James. In England the Renaissance had a character vastly different from the movement in Italy; there the paganism of the Italian Renaissance was modified by the influence of Christianity, particularly Calvinism, and by the ideas of the growing middle class. The new ideas of the sixteenth century affected all of England and changed the social and intellectual qualities of its citizens.

Since ideas are never static, these new concepts underwent continual modification in the seventeenth century, but they carried always a vigorous nucleus derived from Renaissance ideology. Many specific illustrations might be given, but one of the most dramatic and far reaching is the influence of this ideal of the Christian gentleman—an ideal which had greater repercussions on American political and social life than are apparent to the casual observer.

Most emigrants who arrived in America in the first century of settlement, it is true, were neither technically gentlemen nor men of letters. For the most part they were plain folk who came to better their economic lot. But ideas, even abstruse ideas, are not confined to "intellectuals." In our own time, for instance, everybody uses the jargon of twentieth-century Austrian and German psychologists. Repressions, complexes, and neuroses are a part of the common stock of everybody's thinking, but few who use these terms ever read a line from Freud or Jung or even know what they are echoing. Yet these psychological doctrines have affected the lives of most individuals today. In similar fashion, Renaissance doctrines percolated into the consciousness of every type of citizen, and many emigrants who came to America had, in varying degrees, ideals of conduct ultimately derived from Renaissance treatises on the proper behavior of a gentleman.

Whatever these emigrants were by birth and breeding, they hoped to become landowners and substantial members of society. Some were yeomen with a little money saved; others were sons of merchants and tradesmen; a few were really scions of the landed gentry, but all hoped to improve their social status through the acquisition of land. From time immemorial land had been the symbol of aristocracy. In England, where social classes were not frozen into castes, there had always been an upward movement into the landed families through marriage or the purchase of estates as men got richer in various ways. The New World offered undreamed-of possibilities for social advancement because land —the magical basis for gentility—could be had with relative ease.

The colonial period saw the establishment of an upper rank of gentlemen in nearly every region. The landed aristocracy of Virginia and Maryland are the best known, but there were aristocrats equally proud of their positions in South Carolina, Pennsylvania, New Jersey, New York, and New England. The basis of their wealth, and hence of their gentility, varied from locality to locality, but in the seventeenth and early eighteenth centuries these American gentlemen shared a stock of inherited ideals and could be recognized as spiritually akin. John Winthrop and his successors in Massachusetts Bay had more in common with Richard Lee and his successors in Virginia than we have hitherto been accustomed to admit.

A major influence making for similarities in the ideals of the colonial aristocracy was the inheritance from the Renaissance of a strong classical tradition. Sixteenth-century England saw a great emphasis on humanistic training. The goal of education, formal and otherwise, was to develop all sides of man's personality, to make him a thinking citizen and a capable leader because he knew the great traditions of the past.[2] To fulfill this ideal, the Renaissance looked back to the civilizing influence of the Greek and Roman world. Let me emphasize that learning the Greek and Latin languages was not an end in itself, as one is sometimes led to believe. The Renaissance found in the civilizations of Greece and Rome qualities for emulation, and they learned the languages that they might unlock stores of wisdom which otherwise would have remained buried.

From the classics they got their ideal of education for leadership, and in Greek and Roman history and philosophy they found principles of government, ethics, and social relationships which still govern our thinking, though we have forgotten the sources.

The Renaissance ideal of education deserves our thoughtful attention, for that ideal accounts for the quality of a remarkable leadership. And the Renaissance concept of education, in comparison with ours, may raise some questions that today we need to face honestly.

From Aristotle the Renaissance derived four principles that education must seek to induce in men who would be leaders: fortitude, temperance, prudence, and justice. From Christian ethics, the Renaissance got two other principles: liberality and courtesy. These six virtues made up an ideal of conduct desirable for everyone, but particularly for men who would become leaders. And, contrary to general belief, leadership was not the exclusive monopoly of the wellborn. Beginning in the grammar schools and continuing through the universities and the rest of life, these principles received constant iteration; literature and history, for instance, were studied for the illustrations they offered of these six virtues.

The definition of these virtues was not narrow. For example, prudence meant something far more important than the present connotation of caution. Prudence required wide knowledge so that a man could act with wisdom in any emergency. Young men studied the career of Alexander the Great, for instance, not only to learn how he had achieved his successes, but to discover the faults that led to his disasters. Teachers constantly pointed out the lessons to be applied to conditions of their own time. Justice required learning in the principles of law as set forth by Solon and Justinian and study of the manifestations of justice and injustice to be found by diligent reading in the histories of all countries. Our own neglect of history is reflected in the ignorance manifested in the utterances of our lawmakers. No member of Parliament in 1600 would have been guilty of the kind of historical ignorance that has echoed in the halls of Congress during the past few years—an ignorance which has had unfortunate results in governmental policies.

Liberality did not mean merely the virtue of being generous on occasion. The Renaissance ideal of liberality required the cultivation of a liberal and tolerant spirit through the contemplation of human actions, past and present. Courtesy meant something more than saying "Thank you" and replying to invitations on the right kind of stationery; courtesy required a knowledge of human relations in each stratum of society and taught men how to adapt themselves to the demands of any sort of human contact. Fortitude and temperance were positive as well as negative virtues. To demonstrate courage and to control one's self became the mark of the man capable of leadership.

Renaissance education had a single purpose: to induce the qualities that exemplified the six virtues I have mentioned. The goal was not to produce a race of pious prigs, but to train a body of men ready and eager to serve the state in the most intelligent fashion. The state itself, unlike the Nazi state, was conceived in Grecian terms. It was a state that had for its dream the highest cultivation of the individual. But the individualism of the Renaissance was not a detached individualism of anarchy; on the contrary, it made possible the cultivation of man's full powers under the restraints of law.

9

The American Writer and the European Tradition

Whether the colonial aristocrat was a Puritan merchant of Boston, an Anglican tobacco planter on the James River, or a planter-trader of Charleston, South Carolina, he retained the old faith in classical learning as a way to wisdom, and he subscribed to the virtues of Aristotle, modified by Christian ethics, as a code of conduct.

To what extent Renaissance gentlemen—or colonial gentlemen—actually lived up to the code is a question hard to answer. But in any age the acceptance and persistence of a high ideal is significant, even if few or none approach perfection in its practice. And we do know that both in sixteenth-century England and in colonial America there were many examples of men noted for their adherence to this ideal of behavior.

Sir Philip Sidney would have found Richard Lee an understanding and compatible friend. Both were learned men, with their education out of the same books; both were zealous in their service to the state and placed their duty to the commonwealth ahead of personal gain or glory; both were bookish men but at the same time were equally men of action. More than a century in time and an ocean in space separated these two, but they had the same outlook. If it is objected that there were few Philip Sidneys or Richard Lees, we must answer that there were many only a little less distinguished for the practice of the same virtues.

Richard Lee's life illustrates two significant characteristics of the colonial gentleman: he felt an obligation to be learned and an equal obligation to serve the state. When he died, his tombstone recorded in impeccable Latin that "while he exercised the office of magistrate he was a zealous promoter of the public good. He was very skilful in the Greek and Latin languages and other parts of polite learning. He quietly resigned his soul to God, whom he always devoutly worshiped, on the 12th day of March, in the year 1714, in the 68th year of his age."

Here was a man, living in the wilderness of Westmoreland County, Virginia, who was careful to keep up his learning, to set an example in religion, and to fulfill his civic duties. Governor Spotswood testified that Lee was "a gentleman of as fair charac-

ter as any in the country for his exact justice, honesty, and un-
exceptionable loyalty in all the stations wherein he has served
in this government." And a grandson observed somewhat sor-
rowfully that his ancestor had been learned but had not made the
most of his opportunities to improve his patrimony: "Richard
spent almost his whole life in study, and usually wrote his notes
in Greek, Hebrew, or Latin . . . so that he neither diminished
nor improved his paternal estate . . . He was of the Council in
Virginia and also other offices of honor and profit, though they
yielded little to him."[3] He might also have added that this
scholar was no cloistered soul, but in addition to other civic
duties, he served as colonel of the militia, and he was a diligent
overseer of his plantation and business affairs. This combination
of the active and contemplative life would have pleased Vittorino
da Feltre or any other Renaissance educator.

Robert "King" Carter (1663–1732) of Corotoman, whose pro-
lific heirs have multiplied until they are legion, was less unselfish
in his devotion to the commonwealth, but he shared many of
Lee's attitudes. For example, he regarded the Renaissance tradition of education as essential to the proper education of youth.
He was so conservative that he regretted that his sons' schoolmaster no longer taught from William Lily's Latin grammar—
the textbook which Shakespeare studied—and he prescribed that
his son Landon should "be made a perfect master" of John
Comenius' *Linguarum Trilinguis* in Latin, English, and Greek.
Classical learning, to this realistic American of the early eighteenth century, meant something more than ornament and osten-
tation. In the wisdom of the ancients he believed his sons would
find lessons which would give them balance and symmetry as
men and citizens.

Robert Carter is sometimes remembered in Virginia history for
his acquisitiveness, for his engrossing of land, for his proud and
haughty spirit—not qualities to endear him to his contemporaries or to later chroniclers. But those faults represent only one
aspect of a versatile and complex character. If Carter was land-
greedy, he was also conscious of his duties to the commonwealth,

11

and at the expense of time, energy, and money, he served his country as a member of the House of Burgesses, as one of the Council of State, as a judge of the county court, as commander of the militia in Lancaster and Northumberland counties, and as naval officer of the Rappahannock River.

Carter also served his God with piety if not humility. As the leading citizen of Christ Church parish, he was the main support of the church, and on Sunday he occupied the most conspicuous pew. His Anglican faith was tempered with rational common sense. Concerning the religious instruction of his sons, he once wrote: ". . . as I am of the Church of England way, so I desire they should be; but the highflown, up-top notions, and the great stress that is laid upon ceremonies, any farther than decency and conformity, is what I cannot come into the reason of. Practical godliness is the substance; these are but the shell."[4] For a man of Carter's spiritual inheritance, religion was essential for a well-rounded personality, for the complete man. His religious ideas would have been approved by the devotees of Queen Elizabeth's *via media*. Though his sixteenth-century theology was tempered somewhat by rationalism, Carter retained much that was Elizabethan in his religious life.

Robert Carter, sometimes described as a cold-blooded landgrabber, was deeply concerned that Virginians might have opportunities for education at home. He had sent his own sons to England for their schooling and he knew something of the privation and danger which this entailed. For that reason he used his influence to foster the development of the College of William and Mary. He served as trustee, member of the board of visitors, and rector, and he founded a scholarship there. Significantly, his tombstone recorded first among his honors that while he served as "rector of William and Mary, he sustained that institution in its most trying times."[5]

Though Carter was intent upon the architecture of his fortune, upon the establishment of his family with a substantial foundation of land, he was not exclusively a materialist. He had that sense of responsibility to society which had become a tradition in England generations before him and which Englishmen in America were at some pains to transmit to posterity.

Even so worldly and so ambitious a social climber as William Byrd II (1674–1744) of Westover exemplified in many respects the Renaissance tradition. Byrd was a busy man of affairs. From his hard-trading father, he had inherited a fortune in land and property which he augmented and improved. Inordinately ambitious and more than a little vain, he spent much time during his periods of residence in England currying favor with noble lords and cultivating the great. Far from exemplary in his personal conduct, he made little effort to resist feminine wiles, and his record of amours would have made Casanova envious. Yet, with all his faults, Byrd transcended dilettantism and self-indulgence to become one of the hardest working and most useful citizens of the commonwealth. At great personal cost in money, time, and energy, he served the province as agent in England and fulfilled many civic duties at home. And throughout a long life he set himself a regimen of study that would have appalled many a cloistered scholar. Byrd would have been at ease with Cosimo de Medici—whom he resembles in some respects—or with Erasmus of Rotterdam, or William Linacre, or Sir Thomas More. The great tradition of humanism saved Byrd from wasteful frivolity and consuming selfishness.

Byrd's diary, which he kept during most of his adult life, describes the daily regimen of a man who forced himself to keep up his learning despite the encroachments of a thousand routine duties. "I rose at 5 o'clock," reads an entry for April 27, 1710,

and read a chapter in Hebrew and some Greek in Homer. Then I went to Council where my warrants passed and several other matters of consequence were done. About 12 o'clock I ate some tongue and then we tried an unfortunate man who had against his will killed his nephew and he was found guilty of manslaughter. I was appointed commander-in-chief of two counties. . . . About 5 o'clock we dined. I ate roast beef for dinner. Then we sat in Council till 9 o'clock. I had good health, good thoughts, and good humor, thank God Almighty, and said my prayers.

Rarely does an entry in the diary fail to note his reading of

13

Hebrew, Greek, Latin, or some modern language. Year in and year out, he set for himself a systematic program of study of the languages which unlocked the best of sacred and classic literature. The diary describes his labors in the service of the state and his zeal to maintain the decorum in religion expected of a gentleman. If at times it also reveals the weakness of the flesh which too often betrayed Byrd, it makes perfectly clear his own remorse and regret over a failure to live up to a great ideal.[6]

Specific illustrations from Virginia and from other colonies might be multiplied indefinitely. The aspirations of a colonial aristocracy to duplicate the culture of an earlier period were responsible for a race of leaders in America who were particularly influential in the eighteenth century. They earnestly believed that privilege carried with it responsibility to society, a concept frequently forgotten in the nineteenth and twentieth centuries. These ideals, traceable to the Renaissance and to classical sources, help to explain the qualities of the more intellectual and more unselfish leaders in the American Revolution and the generation thereafter. One can make a good case for the assertion that Thomas Jefferson was the culmination of the Renaissance tradition in America.

Every American ought to study the life and personality of Thomas Jefferson with thoughtful application. This can be done by reading a good biography and then turning to Jefferson's own writings, especially his letters. A perceptive reader will discover that Jefferson was the kind of man who would have been at home with Erasmus or Vittorino da Feltre or Philip Sidney. He was versatile, ingenious, learned, hospitable, and tolerant. He was withal a gentleman, in everything that word connotes. He cultivated every side of his personality. He was a man of learning, a gracious host and conversationalist, a philosophic thinker, a scientist, a first-class architect, a statesman, and a man of the world.

In our time it has been fashionable among certain dogmatists to deride the political idealism of Jefferson, to call his conception of democratic society and democratic government old-fashioned, out of date, and unworkable in a mechanized age of urban concentration. Such critics either forget or deliberately overlook one of the chief corollaries of Jefferson's political philosophy: that government ought to provide the greatest opportunity for the development of the individual under the restraints of law. That, let me point out, was also an ideal of the English Renaissance.

Jefferson also constantly insisted upon another Renaissance concept: that the individual citizen must be ever conscious of his own responsibilities to society, that privilege and position entail obligations to the state.

College students ought to be particularly attentive to the example and the teaching of Thomas Jefferson. A sound and democratic state, he believed, would require leaders of versatility and learning. He planned an educational system which would give an opportunity to every child in accordance with his capacities. He believed in an aristocracy of intelligence and talents. He believed that modern science and practical knowledge could be fused with classical learning to train men and women to be useful citizens. He believed that every individual has an obligation to himself and to the state to cultivate his mind and talents for the good of society. Jefferson, in his beliefs and in his personal practice, exemplified the best in the tradition which he had inherited from Renaissance England.

Notes

[1] Christopher Marlowe, *The Tragical History of Dr. Faustus* (1588), Scene I, lines 54–55, 77–82, 93–95.

[2] A few paragraphs here are adapted from the writer's previously printed essay, "Humanistic Education and the Democratic State," *South Atlantic Quarterly*, vol. 42, pp. 142–53 (1943).

[3] For details of Lee's life see Louis B. Wright, *The First Gentlemen of Virginia* (San Marino, Calif.: The Huntington Library, 1940) 212–34.

[4] *Ibid.*, 253–54.

[5] *Ibid.*, 251.

[6] See *The Secret Diary of William Byrd of Westover, 1709–1712*, ed. Louis B. Wright and Marion Tinling (Richmond, Va.: Dietz Press, 1941).

The Enlightenment and the American Dream

ANY attempt to define either "The Enlightenment" or "The American Dream" in a reasonably adequate way is doomed to failure or to an expenditure of time far greater than we can afford here. These terms are among the broadest and vaguest generalizations of cultural history. Nevertheless, as the Preacher says, there is a time to keep silence and a time to speak, and this happens to be a time to speak even if one is forced to use unsatisfying terms.

The Enlightenment is what happened to the thinking of men in the Western world between the Renaissance and the early part of the nineteenth century—in that era which is sometimes called the Age of Reason. It is the sum of the ideas of such men as Bacon, Hobbes, Locke, Newton, Descartes, Montesquieu, Voltaire, and Rousseau. It is the period of the New Science, of deism, of natural rights and natural philosophy, of primitivism and the idea of progress. Its distinguishing mark, perhaps, is a new emphasis upon the good in man, of which the corollary is that man has the power, through his intelligence and his industry, to improve his lot by ever greater control of his environment.

Much is to be said for the thesis that philosophy is at bottom a matter of temperament. If we tend to see the ignorance, the selfishness, the sometimes mysterious perverseness of our companions, we have no trouble accumulating evidence of the weakness of human nature, and we find congenial such ideas as the Fall, original sin, the necessity of divine grace, and the inevitability of social control, discipline, and indoctrination. If, on the other hand, we tend to admire the intelligence, the generosity, the sometimes surprising good will of our neighbors, we are then likely to think that this is a pretty good world in spite of all its faults, and to find congenial such optimistic ideas as perfectibility, social progress, democratic government, and self-reliance.

In the period of the Enlightenment, Europeans tended to be temperamentally optimistic. They had confidence in themselves and in their world. Even Newton's demonstration that the solar system moved with a regularity describable in mathematical formula did not humiliate them; on the contrary they saw in such a reduction of the universe to mechanism a great triumph of human reason. Eighteenth-century Europeans looked forward, not backward. From this distance they sometimes seem naive, and many of their fundamental assumptions appear untenable.

The American Dream is, in one sense, an integral part of the Enlightenment. It is the notion that here, on the North American continent, men and women were to make a fresh start, to build a new life and new institutions, free of the cramping restrictions of hallowed customs and vested interests. Here they were to build a society better than any the world had ever seen. The American Dream took shape with the discovery of what was happily called the New World. Different men have of course envisioned the future in different and sometimes incompatible ways. Captain John Smith and Governor William Bradford were in some ways poles apart, as were John Cotton and Roger Williams, John Eliot and John Wise, John Adams and Thomas Jefferson, Alexander Hamilton and Thomas Paine, but all of them were American Dream-ers. There is room in the American Dream for both of the temperamental extremes that have been mentioned. On the whole, however, the prevailing pattern of the American Dream has been that optimistic pattern which characterized the Enlightenment. Its underlying philosophy is embedded in a few magic words which have been used so frequently and for so many purposes that, like table silver, they often seem tarnished.

The chief master of these words was perhaps Jefferson, who set down the self-evident truths of the Declaration of Independence: "that all men are created equal; that they are endowed by their Creator with certain inalienable rights; that among these are life, liberty, and the pursuit of happiness; that to secure these rights, governments are instituted among men, deriving their just powers from the consent of the governed . . ."[1] Again, in his first inaugural, Jefferson described Americans as entertaining "a due sense of our equal right to the use of our own faculties, to the acquisitions of our industry, to honor and confidence from our fellow citizens, resulting not from birth but from our actions and their sense of them."[2]

Like the Enlightenment, the American Dream in these latter days has been regarded sometimes with condescension, as unsophisticated and misguided optimism. The philosophers have told us that liberty and equality are antithetical ideas, daily less likely to achieve balance in an industrialized and interdependent world. The psychologists have demonstrated both that men are unequal intellectually and that great masses of them are so inferior in mental equipment that they cannot even recognize their own best interests. The analysts of public opinion have shown that the consent of the governed can be manufactured by astute propaganda, and have thereby undermined the faith, always perhaps a little mystical, that a majority vote reflects a trustworthy collective wisdom.

The Enlightenment and the American Dream, taken together, present a problem remarkably like that of the hen and the egg. Without the American Dream, there might easily have been no Enlightenment. Without the Enlightenment, the American Dream could scarcely have assumed the shape it did. The one is a part of the other; Jefferson, Paine, and Franklin are central to both. We are dealing, in short, with a nexus, an intertwining of ideas so tangled that it would be foolhardy to speak with assurance on the points which these papers seek to explore. What was the heritage from Europe? What was indigenous (or nearly so) to America? These are questions next to impossible to answer. Let us look, however, at three characteristic concepts of the eighteenth-century mind—the concept of equality, the concept of a government of checks and balances, and the concept of social planning—and attempt to determine what is American about them, and what is European.

One encounters the idea of equality everywhere in America, even in musical comedy. You may remember the character in *Oklahoma* who says that while she does not claim to be any better than anyone else she is damn well just as good. Where did this idea come from?

At the beginning of the seventeenth century, few persons seem to have believed that the way to choose governors or to settle courses of collective action was to ask the butchers, the bakers, and the candlestickmakers to stand up and have their votes counted. Plato and Aristotle had said, to be sure, that political sovereignty rests ultimately with the people; Cicero and others had written of a law of nature in which may be discerned the germ of the idea of inalienable rights; and Hubert Languet, a Huguenot, had asserted the right of revolution in certain circumstances. The British, moreover, had been developing for centuries their common-law and constitutional guarantees. But the Greeks had found better forms of government than democracy, and the prevailing thought of the Renaissance was decidedly aristocratic. Stratification or degree was the dominant idea; it is expressed succinctly in the famous speech by Ulysses in Shakespeare's *Troilus and Cressida* (Act I, Scene iii):

> How could communities,
> Degrees in schools, and brotherhoods in cities,
> Peaceful commerce from dividable shores,
> The primogeniture and due of birth,
> Prerogative of age, crowns, sceptres, laurels,
> But by degree, stand in authentic place?
> Take but degree away, untune that string,
> And, hark! what discord follows . . .

It is small wonder, then, that Governor John Winthrop of Massachusetts Bay, brought up in the tradition of the Christian gentleman, and fortified by the Calvinist certainty of the de-

praved nature of man, should begin his *Modell of Christian
Charity* in 1630 with this axiom: "God Almightie in his most
holy and wise providence hath soe disposed of the Condicion of
mankinde, as in all times some must be rich some poore, some
highe and eminent in power and dignitie; others meane and in
subieccion."[3] "Democracy," wrote the Reverend John Cotton in
1636 in an often quoted letter to Lord Say and Seal, "I do not
conceyve that ever God did ordeyne as a fitt government eyther
for church or commonwealth."[4]

Nevertheless, New England produced in 1717 an important
defense of democracy as a political philosophy: John Wise's
Vindication of the Government of New-England Churches. Man,
said Wise, whatever his moral condition after the Fall, "remains
at the upper-end of Nature" and is "a Creature of a very Noble
Character." To believe that "Nature actually Invests the Wise
with a Sovereignty over the weak; or with a Right of forcing them
against their Wills" is the greatest of absurdities; nature has "set
all men upon a Level and made them Equals."[5]

Wise tells his readers frankly that he got these ideas from the
De Jure Naturae et Gentium of Samuel von Pufendorf, a German jurist whose book, published in 1672, may reasonably be
claimed as a product of the Enlightenment. If John Locke's
treatises on government had been available to Wise, they might
as easily have been his source.

Experience as well as theory, however, must be taken into account in explaining such rebellion against the tradition of degree. Wise was a Congregationalist, and he had behind him nearly a century of democratic practice within the New England
churches, a practice bolstered, moreover, by the Covenant Theology, that form of Calvinism which the Pilgrims and Puritans
brought with them to Massachusetts, and which contained the
germ of the compact theory of the origin of society. Even Cotton
had written, in 1645, a book with the significant title of *The
Way of the Churches of Christ in New-England, or the Way of
Churches Walking in Brotherly Equalitie.* In it he had observed:

it is evident by the light of nature, that all civill Relations are founded in Covenant. . . . there is no other way given whereby a people (sui juris) free from naturall and compulsory engagements, can be united or combined into one visible body, to stand by mutuall Relation, fellow-members of the same body, but onely by mutuall Covenant; as appeareth between husband and wife in the family, Magistrates and subjects in the Commonwealth, fellow citizens in the same city.[6]

The idea of equality was fostered even more, perhaps, by the basic circumstances of American life. Here, said Captain John Smith in *A Description of New England* in 1616, were "no hard Landlords to racke vs with high rents, or extorted fines to consume vs . . . here euery man may be master and owner of his owne labour and land; or the greatest part in a small time."[7] Over and over again the promotion tracts make the point that in America an ordinary man may hunt and fish as freely as a gentleman may in England—and with better success.

It would seem fair to say then, on this matter of equality, that the theory of the Enlightenment sustained the practice of Americans, and that Wise was using Pufendorf as much to give the sanction of authority to his temperamental and representative convictions as for any other reason. It can hardly be argued that the idea of equality is indigenous to America, but it is equally difficult to demonstrate that it has been derived from any single strand of European thought.

A similar complication crops out in even the most superficial examination of American constitutional theory. The American Dream at the Constitutional Convention of 1787 was of a stable, orderly future, and the result, as everyone knows, was the elaborate mechanism designed to make sure that no element of government should be too strong. A legislature of two houses, an executive chosen by an electoral college, a supreme court and a system of inferior courts, together with a division of sovereignty between the central government and the several states—these are institutions with which we are all familiar. Where did they come from?

21

It has been customary to attribute the popularity of the doctrine of checks and balances, which the Constitution reflects, to Montesquieu, whose *L'Esprit des lois,* first published in 1748, is one of the classics of the Enlightenment. Montesquieu admired both the political institutions of Great Britain, as they had taken shape over a long period of time, and the world-view of Newtonian science. The closest American parallel to Montesquieu's thought is that of John Adams. The most casual handling of *A Defence of the Constitutions of Government of the United States of America against the Attack of M. Turgot,* published in three volumes in 1787 and 1788, or of the *Discourses on Davila* of 1790, will convince anyone of Adams' acceptance of some of the characteristic assumptions of the Enlightenment (although confidence in human nature is not one of them). "The vegetable and animal kingdoms," wrote Adams in the *Defence,*

and those heavenly bodies whose existence and movements we are as yet only permitted faintly to perceive, do not appear to be governed by laws more uniform or certain than those which regulate the moral and political world. Nations move by unalterable rules; and education, discipline, and laws, make the greatest difference in their accomplishments, happiness, and perfection.[8]

The "whole mystery of a commonwealth," remarked Adams in the same treatise, consists in "dividing and equalizing forces," in "controlling the weight of the load and the activity of one part by the strength of another."[9] Analogies of this kind in the work of Adams led Woodrow Wilson to assert that the government of the United States "was constructed upon the Whig theory of political dynamics, which was a sort of unconscious copy of the Newtonian theory of the universe."[10]

Once more, however, it would be incautious to say that the Enlightenment is the whole story. The Greek and Roman political philosophers mention the concept of equilibrium; British parliamentary procedures and prerogatives took root early in the colonial legislatures; the seventeenth-century discussion of church government has some relevance to the problem. Consider the following statement:

In common-wealths, it is a Dispersion of severall portions of power and rights into severall hands, joyntly to concurre and agree in acts and processe of weight and moment, which causeth that healthful κρασις and constitution of them, which makes them lasting, and preserves their peace, when none of all sorts find they are excluded, but as they have a share of concernment, so that a fit measure of power or priviledge, is left and betrusted to them. And accordingly the wisdome of the first Constitutors of Common wealths is most seene in such a just balancing of powers and priviledges, and besides also in setting the exact limits of that which is committed unto each; yea, and is more admired by us in this than in their other Lawes . . .[11]

The date here is 1644; the quotation is a part of the address of two English Puritan divines to prospective readers of John Cotton's *The Keyes of the Kingdom of Heaven,* a work which applies the theory of division of power, and to some degree that of checks and balances, to Congregationalism.

Here, as in the case of equality, the contribution of the Enlightenment would seem to be a new emphasis, a new authority. Montesquieu and Adams appear to have developed, in new phraseology and with new analogies, ideas already latent both in theory and in experience.

A third and perhaps the most controversial aspect of the American Dream relates to the means by which the good society is to be attained. Despite the strongly individualistic flavor of American thought, Americans have over and over again turned to legislation as the method of changing and improving their condition. This tendency has clashed, as in the case of the Prohibition experiment, with some cherished liberties, but it is still with us. Where did we get the notion that the good life could be legislated?

Sumptuary laws, regulating personal expenditures and directed against extravagance and luxury, were tried by the Romans, by Charlemagne, and by the English during the fourteenth century when, in the reign of Edward III, the wearing apparel of every class in the nation was prescribed, together with the amount and quality of food that a person could eat. Similar laws were passed occasionally in the colonies, either under the pressure of Puritanism and its opposition to "finery" or because of particular economic stresses. From mercantilism, moreover, the colonies inherited a nationalistic view of commerce which included a readiness to regulate trade. These trends, however, were scarcely the equivalent of what we now call social planning.

The New Science would seem to have contributed to the Enlightenment two concepts which, although in some ways antithetical, are still of enormous importance to our thinking. The first, that there is an order of nature, with which man interferes at the risk of disaster, became one of the chief supports of the economic philosophy of laissez faire and a great comfort to all defenders of the political and social status quo. The second, that by knowledge of the order of nature man can control his environment, provided part of the justification for experimentation. Free enterprise and collective planning have, in a sense, a common origin.

The most interesting eighteenth-century American book on this matter of social planning is probably Benjamin Rush's *An Inquiry into the Influence of Physical Causes upon the Moral Faculty*, published in 1786. Rush defined the moral faculty as "a capacity in the human mind of distinguishing and choosing good and evil, or, in other words, virtue and vice."[12] The health of the moral faculty, he said, can be measured by men's actions, and since actions "affect the well being of society" it behooves society to see that the moral faculty is cultivated and developed. Cultivation and development can be accomplished by controlling the environment, by experiment, by wise social legislation, and most of all by education.

The extent of the moral powers and habits in man is unknown. It is not improbable, but the human mind contains principles of virtue, which have never yet been excited into action. . . . We feel a veneration bordering upon divine homage, in contemplating the stupendous *understandings* of Lord Verulam and Sir Isaac Newton; and our eyes grow dim, in attempting to pursue Shakspeare and Milton in their immeasurable flights of *imagination*. And if the history of mankind does not furnish similar instances of the versatility and perfection of our species in virtue, it is because the moral faculty has been the subject of less culture and fewer experiments than the body, and the intellectual powers of the mind. . . . Hitherto the cultivation of the moral faculty has been the business of parents, schoolmasters and divines. But . . . the improvement and extension of this principle should be equally the business of the legislator—the natural philosopher—and the physician; and a physical regimen should as necessarily accompany a moral precept, as directions with respect to the air—exercise—and diet, generally accompany prescriptions for the consumption and the gout. To encourage us to undertake experiments for the improvement of morals, let us recollect the success of philosophy in lessening the number, and mitigating the violence of incurable diseases.[13]

Rush, who was a physician, used extensive clinical observations to support his view that, since physical causes influence the memory, the imagination, and the judgment, they probably also influence men's capacity of distinguishing between right and wrong. He lists the "pure mechanical" causes which operate upon morals as climate, diet, drink, hunger, disease, idleness, excessive sleep, pain, cleanliness, solitude, silence, music, pulpit eloquence, odors, light and darkness, airs, and medicine. There are also some causes of a "more compound" nature, such as imitation, habit, and association.

Note what is implied by this discussion. The individual, if Rush's position is accepted, has little or no moral choice. If he chooses the vicious rather than the virtuous course he does so because of the physical environment with which he is surrounded. That environment can be changed. Experiments can be made, and their results assessed, until, in the end, the diseases which have their source in ethics can be treated with some knowledge comparable to that which the physician has at his command in the treatment of a pathological condition. This is perhaps the most breath-taking idea of the Enlightenment, and in some respects it is our most important heritage from that period.

Rush was not a great thinker, but he was a rather original one. His French contemporaries, notably Condorcet, were proclaiming the perfectibility of human nature more eloquently, but it was to be another generation or more before sociological science began to take shape. Meanwhile Rush had helped to set in motion most of the characteristic American social reform movements which turned to legislation as the means of achieving their ends: state-supported education, legal and political rights for women, the abolition of slavery, temperance. He even looked forward to socialized medicine.

These three instances must suffice to suggest that the Enlightenment contributed substantially to the American Dream, but that it cannot be regarded as the whole explanation of what Americans have sought to achieve. The idea of equality, one of the fundamentals of democratic thought, was latent in Covenant Theology and Congregationalism, supported by the circumstances of American life, and given much of its form by the new emphasis of the Enlightenment upon the good in man. The idea of political balance, basic to the respect for constitutional government, was a very similar mixture of the old and the new, the foreign theory and the native experience. The idea of social planning, with the use of legislation to improve man's lot by control of his environment, was perhaps somewhat more indigenous, but it too was powerfully supported by the prevailing temper of the Age of Reason.

The importance of these matters hardly needs demonstration. We have all witnessed national elections, conducted under a constitution framed in the eighteenth century. Approximately sixty million Americans cast their votes in accordance with the eighteenth-century theory that the butcher, the baker, and the candlestickmaker are, politically, as wise as Walter Lippmann and David Lawrence. We have all heard endless discussions about the soundness of this theory, in the light of what we know about mass communication and propaganda, the actual control of the political parties which nominate candidates for public office, the electoral college, and various other factors which limit the freedom of choice of the electorate. We shall all continue to hear bitter debate on the true role of government, the dangers of executive and bureaucratic rule, the pros and cons of planning. Generations pass, but the basic issues of life, and the ideas which men and women bring to bear upon those issues, remain remarkably stable, even though the frames of reference which give those ideas meaning may change greatly.

We have learned recently that under the Fascist regime John Steinbeck's *The Grapes of Wrath* was permitted to circulate on the theory that it would convince Italians of the degeneracy of the United States. Instead, the young men, or some of them, concluded that a government which would permit such a novel to appear must have something admirable about it. The moral, it seems to me, is that Americans appear at their best to the rest of the world when they are self-critical. The charming thing about both the Enlightenment and the American Dream is their dissatisfaction with what is and what has been. No one who reads *Candide* will ever again think that this is the best of all possible worlds. No one, I think, who reads widely in American literature will be either smug or chauvinistic.

Notes

[1] Saul K. Padover, *The Complete Jefferson* (New York: Duell, Sloan & Pearce, 1943) 28.

[2] *Ibid.*, 385.

[3] Perry Miller and Thomas H. Johnson, *The Puritans* (New York: American Book Company, 1938) 195.

[4] *Ibid.*, 209.

[5] *Ibid.*, 261, 263.

[6] *The Way of the Churches of Christ in New-England* (London, 1645) 4.

[7] *Travels and Works of Captain John Smith,* ed. Edward Arber and A. G. Bradley (Edinburgh: John Grant, 1910) 195–96.

[8] *The Works of John Adams,* ed. C. F. Adams (Boston: Little and Brown, 1851) VI, 218.

[9] *Ibid.*, IV, 390–91.

[10] *Constitutional Government in the United States* (New York: Columbia University Press, 1908) 54–55.

[11] Thomas Goodwin and Philip Nye, Foreword to John Cotton, *The Keyes of the Kingdom of Heaven, and Power Thereof* (London, 1644) sig. A2 (2).

[12] *The Selected Writings of Benjamin Rush,* ed. Dagobert D. Runes (New York: Philosophical Library, 1947) 181.

[13] *Ibid.,* 208–9.

ROBERT E. SPILLER

Benjamin Franklin: Promoter of Useful Knowledge

Two broad concepts have been put into our hands as instruments with which to attack the problem of our colonial heritage of European ideas and their indigenous development in America. These are the American version of the Christian gentleman and the American inheritance of ideas of liberty and moral order from the Enlightenment. In order to tie these generalizations and others somewhat more closely to our colonial experience, I shall attempt to give you Benjamin Franklin—from provincial printer to world scientist and cosmopolitan.

In Philadelphia we all love Benjamin Franklin—or at least we assume that we do. Whenever we found a club or a school or a lecture series, whenever we build a hotel or open a new street or establish a foundation or a fellowship, our first thought is to name it the Franklin This-or-That. We have had great men in our time, but they all seem to pale before the recurrent image of this wise and canny old philosopher in homespun; this printer who could talk back to kings; this first Horatio Alger hero with a loaf of bread under his arm; this benevolent father of our city.

Yet most of us carry from our schoolboy reading of the *Autobiography*, "The Way to Wealth," and "The Whistle," an underlying suspicion that Old Ben was a hypocrite who preached a tiresome and opportunist morality and then failed to practice what he preached. Bad teaching is responsible for this impression, and for the failure to realize that Franklin was at heart a satirist and a humorist—an early Mark Twain or an American

29

Swift without the bitterness of either—and that his writings followed the literary conventions of the day. "The Whistle" was a bagatelle written for the amusement of his sophisticated French friends, not a fable for the uplifting of youth. The *Autobiography,* with its calendar of virtues, is the frank and whimsical meditation of an old man on the mistakes and progresses of his own youth, writing at last *The Art of Virtue* that he had always planned. He is of course serious about the cultivation of virtue, and he is a pragmatist in that he believes with William James that virtue, like truth, can be measured only by its workability, but his elaborate system of checks and balances is largely ironical.

"The Way to Wealth" is even more a semiserious and benevolent satire on Franklin himself, his readers, the follies of his times, and human nature. He is here writing, not as from himself, but in the person of that most famous of American fictional creations, the pompous and self-important little almanac-maker Richard Saunders. And Poor Richard is reporting the speech of a popular sage, Father Abraham, whom he saw one day addressing a street-corner crowd on the subject of the oppressive taxes imposed by Pennsylvania's absentee proprietors, the sons of Penn. The piece, which was the preface to the almanac of 1758, opens: "I have heard that nothing gives an Author so great Pleasure as to find his works respectfully quoted by other learned Authors." Richard is justly proud of the anthology of wise saws from his own earlier almanacs that compose the speech of Father Abraham. But Carl Van Doren has recently pointed out that there are many of Richard's aphorisms of a quite contradictory nature which Father Abraham did not quote. Franklin is indulging in a little tour de force and is having a good time with his readers—a fact which they probably appreciated even though, without the contemporary context, we miss his point. He was slyly laughing them out of their worries into a happier and more common-sense attitude. The essay was written on shipboard when Franklin was on his way, as agent of the Pennsylvania assembly, to negotiate with the proprietors in England. The times were tight and feeling was high.

There is nothing more dangerous than satire when it is taken straight. Franklin was a product of the Enlightenment, the age of reason in which common sense was raised almost to the level of deity. It is one of the miracles of our history that we produced in our raw colonial days so perfect an example on the bourgeois level of that ideal sophistication which the polished societies of Europe in the eighteenth century regarded as the highest good. A sense of humor is close kin to a sense of proportion—the ability to see things as they are and the wisdom to make the most of life as it is given.

It is evidence of Franklin's ability to accept life and himself as he found them that, even after he became recognized throughout the world as one of its leading natural philosophers and statesmen, he still insisted on calling himself a printer, because a printer he always was at heart. Two hundred years ago he retired as an active printer-publisher and became a "promoter of useful knowledge." On September 29, 1748, he wrote to his friend Cadwallader Colden of New York: "I, too, am taking the proper measures for obtaining leisure to enjoy life and my friends, more than heretofore, having put my printing-house under the care of my partner, David Hall, absolutely left off bookselling, and removed to a more quiet part of town, where I . . . hope soon to be quite master of my own time." He had reached the ripe old age of forty-two, he had risen from poverty to a reasonable competence, and he was ready to leave the pursuit of living for the pursuit of life. Although he did not know it at the time, he had reached his exact meridian and had a second forty-two years ahead. His life divides precisely in half by this action. He had spent the first half identifying himself completely with his immediate environment, studying life as it was given, putting it to his own best uses, and sucking from it what wisdom it had to offer. He was to spend the second half experimenting with its hidden forces, studying that mind might be superior to matter, controlling the actions of men and nations by his superior understanding of the moral order of nature, and disseminating wisdom throughout the known world.

The decade from 1740 to 1750 tells the story of this change of attitude; in it and in what Franklin did with it, we may perhaps find a key to the problem of our present concern: the growth of American culture from its first roots in American soil to a flowering after three centuries as a dominant world culture. My focus, then, is even narrower than upon a single man. I wish to hold your attention upon the ten years in which the provincial but distinctly American part of his life was completed and the broad and cosmopolitan part was initiated. If we can understand precisely what happened to Franklin in those ten years, we may appreciate more keenly the cyclic process by which a transplanted civilization developed from dependence to independence to dominance.

Let's look first at Franklin the bookseller. One of the last products of his Philadelphia press when he was still in single control of it was a "catalogue of choice and valuable books to be sold for ready money only by Benj. Franklin, at the Post Office in Philadelphia, on Wednesday, the 11th of April 1744, at Nine a Clock in the Morning." This catalogue was recently reproduced in facsimile for the Bibliographical Society of America.

We can see the rows of brown cowhide volumes with their red leather labels, recently arrived from London, with "the lowest Price mark'd in each book." Franklin would, of course, be there promptly on this first day of the sale, a still young and vigorous tradesman who knows his wares. He has not read *all* his books, but they reflect either his own taste or his estimate of the tastes of his public, for they were shipped by his agent William Strahan on specific order. As the good citizens of Philadelphia come in, he has something of interest to discuss with each. Perhaps the elderly James Logan is the first to arrive, and the bookseller tells him that his translation of Cicero's *Cato Major, or His Discourse on Old Age* is being readied for the press and should be out before the end of the year. Would Logan like to see this first draft of the Preface from the Printer to the Reader? Franklin had taken pains to set up "this first Translation of a *Classic* in this *Western World* . . . in a large and fair Character, that those who begin to think on the Subject of Old Age (which seldom happens till their Sight is somewhat impaired by its Approaches) may not, in Reading, by the *Pain* small Letters give the Eyes, feel the *Pleasure* of the mind in the least allayed."

The pleasures of the mind had long since proved their worth in the friendship, in spite of political differences, of these two, for Logan had one of the richest of American colonial libraries, still in existence today as a part of Franklin's Library Company collection, and he doubtless took home on this day as many books as he could carry, from Longinus' *On the Sublime* to a new Graeco-Latin lexicon.

Franklin then welcomes his Junto friend, the ironmonger from Lower Market Street. Yes, the pamphlet on the "new invented Pennsylvania fireplaces"—the celebrated Franklin stove—will be out in November, and both men hope, for different reasons, that the new stove will prove to be popular. Perhaps Dr. Thomas Bond, who with Franklin was soon to found the Pennsylvania Hospital, meanwhile has been over in the corner looking at Brown's *Anatomy of the Muscles*, Cooke's *Marrow of Physics, Surgery, and Anatomy,* and Floyer's *Cold Baths.* Franklin has recently been reading Hales' *Vegetable Statics* and he wants the doctor's opinion on the parallels between the flow of sap in vegetables and of blood in the human veins, a subject he has recently been discussing with his botanist friend John Bartram. Bartram himself soon appears and Franklin does not allow friendship to interfere with the sale of Mortimer's *Husbandry and Gardening* and Clark's *Demonstration of Sir Isaac Newton's Philosophy.*

The quiet conversation is interrupted by the vigorous greeting of the Reverend George Whitefield, the Wesleyan preacher, just back from four years in England, whom Franklin had supported a few years previously in his whirlwind campaigns through the colonies. Whitefield has stopped in to see his American publisher, not so much to buy books, for he is too much on the move to accumulate a library, as to inquire about the sale of his own. He is tempted by the Greek *Apocrypha* on a high shelf; and he compliments Franklin on his fine representation of theological and philosophical works, mainly the more recent critics and rationalists like Shaftesbury, Pufendorf, and Watts.

There is something on these shelves for every interest, although they are stronger in science, in the rationalistic critique of law— natural, theological, and civil—and in history than they are in literature. To be sure, Bacon and Shakespeare, Thomson and Montaigne are here, and Rollin's *Method of Teaching and Studying the Belles Lettres*. The number of books on new methods of study is especially obvious, for Franklin's own skeptical and inquiring mind was an accurate reflection of his time and his place. In 1744, for reasons that are not all as yet discovered, Philadelphia was already becoming the intellectual and social heart of the British colonies scattered along the seacoast. Whether Franklin was a chief cause or a mere reflection of this trend cannot be finally stated, but, in his role of public printer, he did much to make his adopted city "the Seat of the *American* Muses," the capital of the united colonies during the war of rebellion, and the home of the first national government.

Books, Franklin saw clearly, books—new books, old books, imported books, home-printed books, folios, quartos, octavos, leather-bound books, pamphlets, broadsides, magazines, newspapers—were the means to this end. The first need of an indigenous American culture was a firm link with the traditional culture of Western Europe, and the teeming intellectual life of eighteenth-century London had to be transplanted to the busy little colonial port of Philadelphia. In his "Apology for Printers" (1731) he had defended the "vast Unconcernedness as to the right or wrong of Opinions contain'd in what they print" that made printers the agents of the inquiring mind, and a few years later he instructed Strahan not to be "too nice in the Choice of Pamphlets you send me. Let me have everything, good or bad, that makes a Noise and has a Run." But he chose his books carefully, as is illustrated by the wisdom and variety of those listed in his catalogue.

Where did this poor boy with a self-made education acquire the judgment that this list represents? The answer is that Franklin always was a teacher, but like any good teacher, in every action he learned more than he taught. He was capable of absorbing wisdom through the covers of the books he sold and from the customers to whom he sold them. His earlier trips to London had put him in close touch with the printing and bookselling world of that cultural capital, and he kept in touch with it by subscribing to the British journals and importing the best that it had to offer. It is not surprising that his young friend, the watchmaker's apprentice David Rittenhouse (born 1731), became an internationally known astronomer and president of the American Philosophical Society, that another young friend, Benjamin Rush (born 1745), became one of the most distinguished physicians and humanitarians of his day, and that an obscure suburb of his city produced Benjamin West (born 1738), who began his painting, according to legend, by stealing hair from the family cat to make brushes and became the founder and second president of the British Royal Academy. These men grew from the soil that Franklin the bookseller had fertilized.

It might be possible to argue that Franklin was merely feathering his own nest by serving books to the public, were it not that he had, in 1731, founded a rival to his sales in the first American circulating library, the Library Company of Philadelphia, a by-product of his little group of serious apprentice thinkers, the Junto. Would people buy books more or less if they could read them for a small investment in the stock of the company and an annual fee? Franklin obviously argued that anything stimulating reading would be good for his business, and the library throve. Through Bartram he had met (across the water) the English botanist and philanthropist Peter Collinson, with whom Bartram for many years exchanged seeds and roots and plants until the flora of the two English-speaking countries were as alike as the language. Collinson voluntarily became the buyer for the library and guided the selections of Strahan and other booksellers with his own far-ranging knowledge, supplemented by hints from his American friends. "I have receiv'd your several Favors," Franklin wrote him on October 18, 1748, ". . . with all the Books and

Pamphlets you have sent at Sundry Times for the Library Company: We wish it were in our Power to do you or any Friend of yours some Service in Return for your long-continued Kindness to us." The 1835 printed catalogue of that pioneer library lists fifty thousand books. In that one big book is buried the intellectual history of our nation during the entire period of its foundation and early growth.

Franklin knew, many years before our era of "Great Books," that people are what they read, and he salted his own imprint list of official documents, Indian treaties, almanacs, and the *Pennsylvania Gazette* with sermons and religious tracts representing all the Protestant sects, especially the writings by and about the Wesleyan Whitefield and the German Pietist Zinzendorf; with Watts' Hymns and the poems of Aquila Rose; with Blair's *Doctrine of Predestination* and Jonathan Edwards' *Distinguishing Marks of a Work of the Spirit of God*; with Tennet's *Essay on Pleurisy* and home medical manual; with translations of Cato and Cicero; with guides to the English tongue, Dodsley's *Chronicles of the Kings of England,* Bolingbroke's *On the Spirit of Patriotism,* and Cadwallader's *Essay on the West India Dry-Gripes*; and in 1743—just three years after its appearance in London—with the first and most famous of English novels, Richardson's *Pamela.* Even so short a list is phenomenal for a decade or so of colonial publishing and should be judged for its range and variety rather than for its quantity. It determined Philadelphia's pre-eminence as a publishing center for a hundred years. In addition, Franklin initiated the idea of publishing an American monthly on the model of the London *Gentleman's Magazine* and was beaten to the tape by only a few days when his proposed editor took the idea to his rival Andrew Bradford, and two magazines instead of one appeared.

The printer Franklin's multiple role of importer, maker, and purveyor of books—and incidentally of wisdom—was carried on in succeeding generations by Isaiah Thomas, Mathew Carey, George Herbert Putnam, Charles Scribner, and others down to our own Alfred Knopf, William Sloane, John Farrar, and George

P. Brett. This principal link of the young republic with the culture of the Old World has never been severed.

But Franklin was not content to limit his activities as a promoter of useful knowledge to books and printer's ink. Books, after all, may become the mere caskets of wisdom; ideas are wisdom itself, and Franklin, in that same marvelous decade of the forties, founded the American Philosophical Society, the first of our national learned associations, and shaped the policy of the infant University of Pennsylvania. *A Proposal for Promoting Useful Knowledge among the British Plantations in America* (1743) was the inspiration for the first, and *Proposals Relating to the Education of Youth in Pensilvania* (1749) and *Idea of the English School* (1751) for the second. These three pamphlets provide a cornerstone for distinctively American educational thinking from his day to ours, for here the printer becomes the architect of the national mind, the originator of a pragmatic philosophy and method in higher education. Only Jefferson can compete with him in this role, and although Jefferson's scholarly mind carried both theory and program far beyond Franklin's proposals, the two men differed mainly in degree and time. Franklin anticipated Jefferson by a half-century in his emphasis on useful or experimental as distinguished from merely philosophical science, and in his desire to promote general education as a primary function of democratic society.

Carl Van Doren points out that it was mainly his role as postmaster that made Franklin's mind at this time become more intercolonial. He had the opportunity to read the newspapers of colonies other than Pennsylvania and to learn about other men of inquiring mind and about what they did. Among his newer correspondents, for example, was Cadwallader Colden of New York, the author of the *History of the Five Indian Nations* and many treatises on medicine, moral philosophy, and natural science. Franklin himself printed Colden's *Explication of the First Causes of Action in Matter, and, of the Causes of Gravitation* (1745), which attracted much attention by its implied criticism of Newton, and a few years later he also printed Samuel

Johnson's *Elementa Philosophica* (1752), an ethical system by an American philosopher who independently followed the line of British Bishop Berkeley's idealism. It was such men and such thinking that the Philadelphia printer hoped to draw together for their mutual benefit and for the improvement of mankind. In his first *Proposal* he wrote:

The first drudgery of settling new colonies, which confines the attention of people to mere necessities, is now pretty well over; and there are many in every province in circumstances that set them at ease, and afford leisure to cultivate the finer arts and improve the common stock of knowledge. To such of these who are men of speculation, many hints must from time to time arise, many observations occur, which if well examined, pursued, and improved, might produce discoveries to the advantage of some or all of the British plantations, or to the benefit of mankind in general.

Franklin proposed therefore to form a society of *virtuosi* or ingenious men who should meet once a month or oftener in Philadelphia, as a convenient center with a growing library, "to communicate to each other their observations and experiments." To them and to distant members he offered free postage for their communications, and his own services as secretary "till they shall be provided with one more capable." The resident members should always include, he specified, "a physician, a botanist, a mathematician, a chemist, a mechanician, a geographer, and a general natural philosopher." Pure philosophy, logic, rhetoric, the arts and letters are not mentioned.

It would be a mistake, however, to think that Franklin's aims were narrowly utilitarian even though at this time he was publishing pamphlets on fire control, censorship, how to get rich and how to keep healthy, and the military security of the city. In his earlier "Dialogues of Philocles and Horatio" he had stated the belief that "as the Happiness or real Good of Men consists in right Action, and right Action cannot be produced without right Opinion, it behoves us, above all Things in this World, to take care that our Opinions of Things be according to the Nature of Things. The Foundation of all Virtue and Happiness is Thinking rightly," or shaping our opinions in accordance with natural law. This is a form of moral idealism far more profound than the utilitarian and opportunist moralism we so often attribute to him, a moral philosophy derived from the deism of the eighteenth century but not unlike that of the supposedly impractical transcendentalists of the nineteenth. The difference is that Franklin was ahead of his times in emphasizing the pragmatic test of truth, and so is in closer accord with William James and John Dewey than he is with either the Mathers and the Edwardses of his own day or the Emersons and the Alcotts of the intervening century.

Tocqueville's description, in 1835, of the typical American philosophic attitude could be taken as a description of Franklin's or Emerson's or Dewey's alike: "To accept tradition only as a means of information, and existing facts only as a lesson used in doing otherwise, and doing better; to seek the reason of things for one's self, and in one's self alone; to tend to results without being bound to means, and to aim at the substance through the form." Tocqueville is right when he says that "the inhabitants of the United States . . . without ever having taken the trouble to define the rules of a philosophical method . . . are in the possession of one, common to the whole people." Since his day we have defined that method as pragmatism, with its variants, and it is still the characteristic American philosophy, a philosophy which is always a method of thinking and acting rather than an abstract and systematic statement of the ultimates—truth, goodness, and beauty—in the Greek or Germanic fashion. This is what Franklin meant, and what we still mean, by "useful knowledge," a knowledge that can be tested by experiment and application. Whether we like the idea or not, our great universities, in which the college is the germinal center of a group of professional schools rather than, as in England, one of a group of interrelated colleges, are the final and outward expression of this epistemological position.

How then did Franklin arrive at this position when the colonial colleges already established—Harvard, Yale, and William and Mary—as well as the nearly contemporary Princeton, all were built upon an a priori foundation of truth based on theological or traditional authority and classical rhetoric and logic? The answer, of course, is that Franklin was our first intellectual leader to master for himself the wisdom of the Western world and to re-examine it strictly in its applicability to American experience. To him the inheritance of the Enlightenment—revolt as it was in itself from ancient authority—was worthless unless it could be applied in this philosophical sense to the century and more of fresh experience in settling the new continent. In listing the subjects suitable for correspondence among the members of his society, he uses the word *new* eight times in a single paragraph, and the word *method,* with its variants *discoveries, inventions, improvements,* ten. This document, with its reflection of the liberal thought of the Enlightenment, may be taken as the declaration of independence of American science and of the higher learning that we have built upon it.

Two further actions of Franklin, in this decade of the forties, gave a force and a direction to higher education and to research which have shaped our conduct ever since: he founded the University of Pennsylvania, later to be the first state university, with an original and radical "English" school; and he conducted those experiments in electricity which brought him international fame as a scientist and a permanent position in the history of science.

His next two pamphlets, concerned with shaping the institution and the curriculum of the academy in Philadelphia, have already been mentioned. Apparently his connection with the Charity School of 1740, from which the University of Pennsylvania officially dates its foundation, was incidental, and the failure of that school is perhaps due to this fact. Doubtless realizing that a false start had been made, Franklin, in characteristic fashion, sought the working principles upon which an academy for youth should ideally be founded. His *Proposals Relating to the Education of Youth in Pensilvania* was the result, and, again characteristically, the proposals led to action within the year and a near failure was turned into an enduring success.

This was not a school designed to produce gentlemen, statesmen, and clergymen. Rather it was planned to train youth to enter the world and establish themselves, "whether in Business, Offices, Marriages, or any other Thing for their Advantage, preferably to all other Persons whatsoever even of equal Merit." The test again is the pragmatic one of superiority in those attainments and abilities which lead to a satisfying and happy life in a competitive society.

To this end, he proposes patience and kindliness on the part of the masters, in contrast to the usual impersonal sternness, with care for the physical health of their charges. He urges that, because "Art is long, and their Time is short," pupils should learn "those things that are likely to be *most useful* and *most ornamental*," that is, penmanship, arithmetic, the English language and the best English authors (with special attention to style), declamation (with emphasis on pronunciation), ancient and modern history (in translation if necessary), geography of those places "where the greatest actions were done," chronology, ancient customs, morality, and natural history (or science). History, oratory, and experiment should be stressed, and such subjects as botany, commerce, and mechanics built upon the foundations thus laid. Even though Milton had proposed several of these main features in 1644, the plan was still too radical to be carried out in full, but it sketches in broad outline the typical American school and college curriculum of today.

Franklin's experiments in electricity have an educational as well as a scientific significance, for with them he carried his empirical methods to the levels of higher research as we do in our universities now. We are likely to make light of them as contributions to science because scientists in general are not much interested in the early history of their discipline. Furthermore, we are likely to call to mind the picture of a quaint old man out in a thunderstorm with a kite and a key, playing a fine little game for the amusement of grade school children. But in such histories of science as there are, Franklin's name stands in bold type among the earliest experimenters in static electricity; and

41

the terms that he first used, as well as many of the discoveries that he first made, are still rocks at the base of the structure of our knowledge. His experiments were such as to put him shoulder to shoulder with his greatest contemporaries; and experimentation since has modified few of his findings in the field of static, as contrasted to what we may call kinetic, electricity.

The kite experiment was spectacular, and perhaps even dangerous, but it was not historically important except that it demonstrated a fact already known: that lightning is static electricity and that the clouds act as positive and negative poles. Franklin's important work lay in his experiments with the Leyden jar, the simplest and for many years the only known form of condenser, and with the transfer of electricity between charged bodies. He made clear the difference between positive and negative charges of a single "electrical fluid," a hypothesis upon which all subsequent experimentation in currents, waves, electrolysis, radioactivity, and the like has been based. In the history of the subject his name stands in advance of those of Cavendish, Volta, Galvani, and Faraday.

Franklin was forty years old when he became interested in electricity. This was in Boston in the summer of 1746 when the discovery of the Leyden jar by Pieter van Musschenbrock became known to him through a demonstration by a Dr. Spence (r?). During the following winter, Peter Collinson sent to the Library Company an "electric tube," and Franklin immediately set up a series of experiments with it, with the already known "friction machines," and with other equipment of his own invention. He became "totally engrossed" in his studies, both in making experiments when alone and in repeating them for his friends and acquaintances, who, "from the novelty of the thing, come continually in crouds to see them." By July 1747 he was ready to report in a letter to Collinson on "the wonderful effect of pointed bodies, both in *drawing off* and *throwing off* the electrical fire," and to describe his experimental method in detail. This was the first of Franklin's letters on the subject, which were reported by Collinson and others to the Royal Society. They were published in the *Gentleman's Magazine* of 1750–51 and finally in pamphlet form in London in the latter year. Overnight the Philadelphia printer had become the world scientist; but he was already being drawn out of his study by the urgency of the times. He continued his studies for many years, but never again could he devote himself wholly to them as he had in these few happy years.

Franklin had made good his scientific declaration of independence. His eagerness to learn from European experiments, his anxiety to share his own with Hopkinson and others of his Philadelphia friends, and his promptness in reporting his findings to the Royal Society reflect his growth to full stature as a cosmopolitan. His colonial and provincial attitudes had disappeared.

It is not necessary to follow the further development of his cosmopolitanism and to trace his world influence during the years after 1750 because here we are thinking of Franklin not for himself but in order to discover through him the breaking of the American colonial shell, and to distinguish in him those traits which were characteristic of the Enlightenment as a whole from those which were peculiarly American. Intellectual curiosity and skeptical rationalism were obviously shared by him with his European contemporaries, as was a willingness to use, but not merely to take on authority, the accumulated knowledge and opinion of the ages. Franklin went beyond his contemporaries in his desire to make knowledge, both new and old, useful to human welfare, and to extend its experimental resources and its practical applications as well as its theoretical boundaries. His importance lies not so much in his originality as in his ability to absorb the liberal thought of his day, and to put into practice in America those ideas which remained mere theory in the Europe where they originated.

In many ways, this is the American story. Our modern industrial research laboratories as well as our colleges and churches owe much to his identification of the moral with the natural law. The idealist in him gave him a firm basis for the acceptance of moral law; the pragmatist in him pushed him to immediate tests

The American Writer and the European Tradition

for his findings; and the democrat in him made him a promoter as well as a discoverer so that all mankind could be as wise as he. These, it seems to me, are the distinctive traits, not only of Franklin, but of the Americans of his day and of ours. We are an idealistic, a pragmatic, and a democratic people. May we remain so and thus preserve our freedoms.

44

❧ STANLEY T. WILLIAMS ❧

Cosmopolitanism in American Literature
before 1880

"I HAVE BEEN," wrote Washington Irving on August 1, 1841, to his niece, Sarah Storrow, then in Paris, "to a commonplace little church of white boards, and seen a congregation of commonplace people and heard a commonplace sermon, and now cannot muster up anything but commonplace ideas." "Good Lord," he cried, with a frankness absent from his urbane public utterances on America, "deliver me from the all pervading commonplace which is the curse of our country. It is like the sands of the desert, which are continually stealing over the land of Egypt and gradually effacing every trace of grandeur and beauty and swallowing up every green thing."

I enjoy reading this passage to a friend of mine who was reared in the little Pennsylvania village in which Irving wrote this letter, but I have no reason to believe that this highly civilized author, who spent nearly half of his mature years in Europe, regarded Pennsylvania as unique in its commonplaceness. In fact, he says in this amusing letter, in which he envies dear Sarah her "half wicked Parisian Sunday," that in America it is "all pervading." So he felt throughout his entire life. In 1805, studying with Washington Allston in the galleries of Rome; in 1829, setting down sketches in his notebook in the palace of the Alhambra; in 1844, writing his sophisticated letters home from the court of Isabella the Second; and always during his half-reluctant exiles from England and the Continent, he always detested, with all his heart, these "sands" of the American desert.

The American Writer and the European Tradition

So much for the tactful Irving as a critic of "America Philistia"! He was more discreet than others who in their hopes and dreams for the art of letters in our country faced toward Europe; some of these spoke of their native land, on which as artists they had turned their backs, with innuendo, satire, or contempt. We need not quote from them all to establish the force of their criticism of our culture, from Longfellow's weary distaste for books dealing with frontier themes—"Ah," he sighed, as he read Fremont's *Travels,* "the discomforts!"—to Cooper's savage novels on "the wine-discussing, trade-talking, dollar-dollar" Americans.

Instead, we may in this brief introduction to a brief study of the cosmopolitanism in our literature now pass swiftly to the end of the century, to the subtlest, and, after all, the most withering skeptic concerning the possibility, then or ever, of a tolerable life for the artist in America. In listening to Henry James for a moment on this theme we shall not forget his ambivalence, his compensating admiration for certain homespun qualities in America (which form a story other than mine in this paper). Yet, hearing his voice, long after Irving's, we may better understand the persistence in the nineteenth century of our men of letters' distrust of the "all pervading commonplace."

Toward these "sands of the desert" James had attained by his thirty-sixth year a species of horror. In his contemplation of what he considered the tragic handicap of Hawthorne in a country in which even the light upon the fields shone with a certain uncivilized aura, he wrote:

The negative side of the spectacle on which Hawthorne looked out, in his contemplative saunterings and reveries, might, indeed, with a little ingenuity, be made almost ludicrous; one might enumerate the items of high civilization, as it exists in other countries, which are absent from the texture of American life, until it should become a wonder to know what was left. No State, in the European sense of the word, and indeed barely a specific national name. No sovereign, no court, no personal loyalty, no aristocracy, no church, no clergy, no army, no diplomatic service, no country gentlemen, no palaces, no castles, nor manors, nor old

46

country-houses, nor parsonages, nor thatched cottages, nor ivied ruins; no cathedrals, nor abbeys, nor little Norman churches, nor great universities, nor public schools—no Oxford, nor Eton, nor Harrow; no literature, no novels, no museums, no pictures, no political society, no sporting class—nor Epsom nor Ascot! Some such list as that might be drawn up of the things absent in American life—especially in the American life of forty years ago, the effect of which, upon an English or a French imagination, would probably, as a general thing, be appalling. The natural remark, in the almost lurid light of such an indictment, would be that if these things are left out, everything is left out. The American knows that a good deal remains; what it is that remains— that is his secret, his joke, as one may say.

From these introductory quotations we might infer that the causes of facing toward Europe, of the cosmopolitanism in our literature of the nineteenth century, were simple. We might think of this flight of our men of letters from the commonplace as hasty, precious, and a little ridiculous, not unlike the nervous avoidance by the elegant Louis XV of every sign or symbol of death. Are they not akin, these intellectual expatriates, to some "waiting-gentlewoman" (to paraphrase Hotspur) afraid of "guns and drums and wounds," or (to come closer home) to Ichabod Crane, that correct schoolmaster, fleeing headlong before the stalwart Brom Bones? In a word, we are at first inclined to regard this as the retreat of a narrow propriety in literature from reality. It was not so. The causes of cosmopolitanism in our literature were not simple. On the contrary, they were complex; and with these complex causes we shall now be concerned.

The first cause was age-old, less a cause than a hypothesis in human psychology. In their instinctive turning toward Europe American men of letters merely repeated an ancient pattern. In the reign of Henry II, in the twelfth-century Renaissance, Englishmen made the long journey to study in the libraries of Paris; and in later eras other young intellectuals of the Islands buttressed the still insecure literature of Britain by the inspiration of Italy. With or without a competing frontier, the dependence of one literature upon the richer cultural models of another is no newer than the intellectual relationship of Rome and Athens. Thus, when the Irvings in 1804 sent their gifted youngest brother to Rome, to Paris, and to London, the journey was but a version of the eternal "Grand Tour," which we still desire both for ourselves and for our children. Both the excitement of the New England transcendentalists concerning the abounding wealth of Goethe's mind and George Ticknor's and William Hickling Prescott's search through the Peninsula to enrich their own libraries are but illustrations of the law which functions whenever a younger civilization surveys the treasure of an older.

Once recognized as basic to our cosmopolitanism, it is fascinating to observe this law's complete consistency as the frontier moves *westward* and the artist looks ever *eastward,* though now not always as far as Europe! Although the parallel is faulty in detail, we may still perceive in the Territory of Hawaii, despite the presence of a culture far richer than that offered by our own somewhat bleak frontier, the impulse toward the East. The "Era of the Pacific," as new nativists hopefully call it, cannot, in the intellectual life of Hawaii, dull an ardor for the older and more established cultures, for the culture of the "Mainland," of the Eastern Seaboard, and of far-away Europe. Yes, in every phase of the history of our literature we may see the operation of this law. Even in writers whose first experience of life was literally of the soil, we recognize the force of the attraction. Mark Twain's eager search in later life in Europe for a belated knowledge of the fine arts seems to confirm the universal character of this instinct. Our facing toward Europe was less timid, less weak, than it was axiomatic, inevitable for a young and aspiring culture.

If it is true that such dependence is common to all nations during periods of cultural immaturity, we must add that in America this received a special intensification; in American wistfulness toward Europe there is a peculiar quality. For in a sense not true of the relationships of England and Italy or those of Rome and Greece, we had belonged to Europe. Ours was a completely *transplanted* culture; this is a basic second cause for our facing toward the older lands. This fact the young Irving perceived as, from his sailboat on the East River, he watched the ships set out across the Atlantic. What if they carried hardware from the family business? To him they brought back Shakespeare, Rabelais, Cervantes, and Scott, dearer far than all the profits of the Liverpool office. "What," Lowell exclaimed to an Englishman with a letter to Walt Whitman, "What! a letter for Walt Whitman! For God Almighty's sake don't deliver it! Walt Whitman! . . . Why—Walt Whitman is a rowdy, a New York tough, a loafer, a frequenter of low places—friend of cabdrivers!" Likewise, to this student of Chaucer, Milton, Shakespeare, Dante, and Cervantes the strong vascular thought of Thoreau seemed apostasy. The only possible models for the growing literature of the republic seemed to Irving or Lowell those of its own culture, namely Western European. This was true, thought Longfellow, even if by some mischance this culture had drifted across the Atlantic.

This transplanting Lowell never forgot, nor did Longfellow, nor Holmes, nor Prescott, nor Ticknor, nor Hawthorne, content with his "lump" of New England dimly lighted by the lamps of Spenser, Milton, and Bunyan. To these men of letters, even if they were ambitious for a *national* literature, one fact was clear: the roots of our literature were in Europe, and not in Indian saga or the folklore of a dismal frontier. There was no authentic subsoil in America itself: no *Beowulf,* no *Chanson de Roland,* no old romances. These were in Europe. Even the charming eighteenth-century poet, Philip Freneau, whom some of these writers admired as a creator of "early" American poetry, derived from the Western European literature and so, like themselves, ultimately from these primitives of Europe, not from those of the frontier. All these writers would, I think, have subscribed in speaking of the intellectual life of America to an adaptation of Clough's lines:

> By eastern windows only,
> When daylight comes, comes in the light.

Thus to the strong fact, already described, of the magnet of an older culture for a younger, was added this logic of the original transplanting. Irving was to write of the Dutch legends of the Catskills and Longfellow of the Indians, but such writing stemmed from no strong primitive epic or lyric on these themes but from the minds and the reading of half-Europeanized Americans applying the techniques of Europe to fresh material. Thus every natural literary impulse in these early decades of the century led the American blessed with any cultivation not toward the barbarous cultures of Huron or Iroquois but, of course, toward those of his forefathers. Such bonds are not easily broken; they were to outlive mutual contempt, wars, and revolutions. "Our Old Home" was the title of Hawthorne's record of England. I myself am interested, as an illustration of this law, in the parallel of the transplanted Spanish culture in Mexico. In the fresh and brilliant literature of modern Mexico we seem to see elements belying the Spanish origins of the country. In Ramón López Velarde's *Suave Patria* are the corn and the clay and the *mestiza* of his own countryside, and in his other lyrics the stamp of French Symbolism. Be not, however, deceived, says the great Mexican critic, Alfonso Reyes—the ties with Spain are *not* broken. So strong always are the recessive impulses of a transplanted culture.

Such reflections on the intensification of the natural influence of Europe upon our writers lead us inevitably to others on the infinite difference a century ago between the cultural resources of, say, London and Boston. The scales are still uneven, but everywhere we now encounter evidence of our increasing intellectual riches. Simple illustrations are best. At Yale in a little group of students of American culture have appeared from their respective countries a Swiss, a Frenchman, a Swede, and—the order is climactic!—an Englishman. Such a fact symbolizes a shift in balance; more and more, in learning and in literature, Europe looks toward us. But a century ago, how different! In Concord Emerson could not find a German grammar, and Ticknor, returning from abroad, remarked of the Harvard College library: "When I went away I thought it was a large library; when I came back, it seemed a closetful of books."

Stanley T. Williams

The acknowledged superiority of European culture is likewise vividly implied in the jubilation in Boston in 1837 over the appearance of Prescott's *Ferdinand and Isabella*—the universal Christmas present of the year, for the civilized! Here was an event more encouraging than the publication of Irving's *Sketch Book*; here was a scholarly history of inscrutable Spain written by an American, from materials which were, through Prescott's zeal, henceforth to repose in the public and private libraries of Boston. Everywhere American cosmopolitanism was drawing its life from the incomparable cultural resources of Europe. It is well to ask ourselves this question honestly: had we lived in 1837 would we have shared this interest in *Ferdinand and Isabella* or would we have turned to a volume published in the same year, Robert Montgomery's novel, *Nick of the Woods?* This book immediately ran through twenty editions and told the dark and bloody legend of the Kentucky frontier in a fashion which absolved it of any contamination whatever from European culture:

Gentlemen of the Jury . . . what I have to say . . . is . . . that the man thar', Captain Ralph Stackpole, did, in the year seventeen seventy-nine, when this good State of Kentucky . . . [was] overrun with yelping Injun-savages—did, I say, gentlemen, meet two Injun-savages in the woods on Bear's Grass, and take their scalps, single-handed—a feat, gentlemen of the jury, that a'n't to be performed every day, even in Kentucky!

Since the cultural resources of Europe were boundless and since they blended without sharp distinction, in the minds of most Americans, with the outward antiquity of Europe (the cathedral, the thatched cottage, the moated castle), our facing toward Europe received support, in less vigorous minds and in less profound writers, from the accompanying mood of romance. Indeed, this is a fourth factor, and a powerful one, in our literary cosmopolitanism. Eventually the laughter of a Mississippi River pilot was to dispel this romance, but not until it had become a habit of mind strongly affecting cosmopolitanism.

Most writers lacked the practical view of Cooper who thought of Europe, he said, as a place for "my own health and the instruction of my children in the French and Italian languages." For them it was rather the place, as Irving and Longfellow had taught, of "storied association," of castles and beleaguered maidens. It was the place where, in the defiles of the mountains, Alexander Slidell Mackenzie had faced bandits, and where Irving had been captured by pirates—incidents far more romantic, apparently, than Mary Rowlandson's imprisonment by the Indians. We may sense this temper not only in Irving, Prescott, Longfellow, and John Hay, who knew the American frontier, but in hundreds of forgotten or obscure people, of whom Harriet Trowbridge Allen may serve as an example. "I can hardly realize," she wrote, "as yet that we are in Spain . . . I feel at home amid these familiar names, recalling as they do many a story and legend of romance, of knight and cavalier and Moorish warrior."

From this complex, whose component parts we have seen to be the natural attraction of the old civilization for the new, the intensification of this in a transplanted literature, the gigantic cultural resources of Europe, and the romantic haze of far-away lands and bygone days—from all such interrelated convictions and moods arose the conclusion that the man of letters, the artist, could not dwell in America. How could he? It was too difficult. Should he, if a painter, like Washington Allston despair over his unsold pictures? Or, if a writer, like Washington Irving see in the arching forests of the Southwest, with a wave of homesickness, the Moorish arches of Cordova? Or, like Longfellow, turn bourgeois poet for the illiterate masses? Or, in newspaper, preface, and novel (Cooper's *Home as Found,* for instance), fight the "all pervading" commonplace? Or, like Mark Twain and Whitman, turn the strident values of the democracy into a literature which would repudiate art and vulgarize the world?

It was the same story over and over, in the lonely lives of Hawthorne, Lanier, and Emily Dickinson, in the popularity of such a crudity as *The Innocents Abroad,* in the expatriate colonies in Paris and Rome. For the artist America was impossible!

The artist did not require a patron, a subsidy, or the shouts of the republic. But he could not breathe the air of his native land, so choked was it with the dust of Manifest Destiny. In 1852 appeared a memorable picture of the artist's plight in America in books XVII and XVIII of Herman Melville's *Pierre*. More and more, cosmopolitanism included the belief that if the writer could not actually live in Europe, he must at least dwell there in imagination.

Such are the primary causes of our literary cosmopolitanism; without them we should not have looked toward Europe either so long or so fondly. Yet there were other factors, cause-effects I call them, such as travel, which derived from the cosmopolitan spirit and at the same time stimulated it. These we shall study briefly. From the close of the Revolution until the middle of the nineteenth century the returning traveler from Europe was a marked man. Irving's and Emerson's first voyages to Europe cost them, respectively, in sailing ships, thirty-eight and forty days. Travel was arduous; Prescott never ventured into Spain. Yet Irving knew the Spanish novelist Fernán Caballero; in Sweden, Longfellow had seen Tegnér; and Ticknor had met nearly every statesman and man of letters on the Continent.

It is, therefore, impossible to exaggerate the effect upon curious minds of the personal relation by Emerson of his night of "wide talk" with Carlyle or of Irving's description of Abbotsford and Scott. "This," Irving said, "was to be happy. I felt happiness then." "He made his travels," said an envious friend, "go a great way." Examples are innumerable, but whether we think of Bayard Taylor who, an enemy remarked, had traveled more and seen less than any other American, or of Benjamin Silliman, with his forthright record of his stays in England, whether we think of the vast literature of travel books or of the quiet talk in Emerson's study from those who had visited Goethe, we may perceive the strengthening of cosmopolitanism through travel in Europe.

Meanwhile, like a staff for the traveler, flourished the magazine, another related factor in our literary cosmopolitanism. Here the wanderer wrote of his penetration far into Spain, even to the Moorish mosque at Cordova, or of the frescoes in the Vatican, or of his interview with Wordsworth. Still speaking of the first half of the century, it may be said that any reader of the magazines was necessarily a reader concerning Europe: he encountered vignettes of famous men, renowned scenes, with illustrations, and generous selections from European history, poetry, and fiction. As late as 1898 James Russell Lowell published in the *Century Magazine* basic portions of his *Impressions of Spain*. Beginning with the founding of the *North American Review* in 1815, the magazines exerted a continuing influence upon our intellectuals through such articles as Longfellow's on linguistic studies and through reviews and discussions of the writings on Europe by Irving, Ticknor, Prescott, and others. "Our periodicals teem," said the *Western Monthly Review* for July 1829, "with abstracts and reviews of English and German books." It is difficult to see how a brilliant young writer of this era, say one named Poe, reading and editing the magazines, could have escaped entire immersion in the European scene.

Let young Poe serve as an illustration of another phase of literary cosmopolitanism. For included in his curiosity concerning Europe was an interest in its languages. His apprenticeship in French at the University of Virginia reminds us of Jefferson's encouragement of such studies and of his establishment of a professorship of modern languages at William and Mary in 1779. In 1751 Garret Noel had published the first textbook for the study of Spanish. All such incidents were preliminaries to the year 1825 when the overseers of Harvard implemented the Abel Smith professorship with money "to pay the expense of private instruction and recitation in the French and Spanish languages, and in part go to the support of a professor of the Literature, as well as the Languages of these nations."

This was a happy event. For three quarters of a century this professorship remained the center from which flowed the dynamics of the study of modern languages. Moreover Ticknor, Longfellow, and Lowell were all, in their own right, men of letters as well as scholars. Bryant, Irving, Prescott, and Lowell spoke Spanish with some skill; Ticknor spoke this language and also French and German. Longfellow spoke all of these, and Italian, too. The marrow of a nation's culture is its language. By 1875 popular instruction in modern European languages was widespread. Thus cosmopolitanism had become more respectable; it had won the support of the scholars. Traveler, editor, teacher —all looked, along with the men of letters, toward Europe.

From this union of learning with cosmopolitanism ensued, besides the solidifying of its temper, two results. One is symbolized by Emerson's reading of Goethe in the original, after exhortations from Carlyle and instructions from Charles Follen, that priceless German émigré and instructor at Harvard. Indeed, the originals of this great German, of Dante and Cervantes (side by side with Shakespeare) now appeared on the tables of cultivated families. Cosmopolitan curiosity was to enjoy more substantial fare than the European soufflé of travel and reminiscence in the magazines. There is truth and wit in Frederick Henry Hedge's address before the Phi Beta Kappa Society in 1828:

> Turn we from these to shapes of other mould,
> Let foreign climes their varied stories unfold;—
> And German horrors rise in dark array,
> And German names more horrible than they.
> Amazed we hear of Werke and Gedichte,
> Of Schlegel, Schleiermacher, Richter, Fichte,
> And thou great Goethe, whose illustrious name,
> So oft mis-spelt and mis-pronounced by fame,
> Still puzzles English jaws and English teeth,
> With Goty, Gurrte, Gewter, and Go-ethe.

The other result of this meeting of the scholar and the cosmopolitan was the multiplication of the translations of foreign masterpieces by these learned men, from the Spanish classics in Ticknor's *History of Spanish Literature*, from Italian poetry in Longfellow's translation of Dante. Nor may we neglect longer Bryant's charming versions of the Spanish religious poets.

Finally, one other crosscurrent of influence deserves our fleeting attention. As America has expanded under its peculiar social liberalisms, there have been flung up within its borders islands, so to speak, of Europe. By ancestry, tradition, and custom, England is of course everywhere, but, more particularly, Sweden is in Delaware and Minnesota, Germany in Pennsylvania, France in Louisiana, and Spain in Florida, Texas, the Southwest, and California. Without the proximity of foreign lands which makes for the internationalism of a Frenchman or a German, America has, nevertheless, in certain areas, long been reminiscent of Europe.

In a few writers this fact intensified the cosmopolitan attitude. We may read of Irving's delight as, traveling down the Mississippi to New Orleans, he heard again in a French village the language and songs he loved. Was he not again young and in Languedoc? And, having stumbled on the incident, we do not forget Bryant in Florida, already in love with Spanish poetry, listening to the songs to the Virgin brought long before by the inhabitants from far away Minorca. The most arresting example of such secondary influences of Europe is the story of Bret Harte, which one day I propose to tell. Fascinated, Bret Harte studied the dress, the speech, and the characters of the Castilian families of California. In such an incident is an amusing paradox: cosmopolitanism on the frontier!

Such patterns, then, intertwined and fused, we may discern in the labyrinthine tapestry of literary cosmopolitanism. Obviously no one writer was influenced by all of these. Yet no writer, no major writer before 1880, which is the theoretical time limit of this essay, not even Whitman or Mark Twain, escaped them all. We recall Whitman's allegiance to Carlyle and Mark Twain's devotion to Browning. It would be almost as exciting as it would be time-consuming to measure, as with Thoreau's graduated snowstick, the vigor and the scope of these cosmopolitan influences upon *all* our men of letters, or upon twenty, or upon ten— so interesting is it, in the light of the different psychology today, to conjecture on the thoughts of a cosmopolitan man of letters in 1850. How could Longfellow embalm so sweetly and so blindly the great themes of the Indian? Why did not the perceptive Lowell divine the greatness of Thoreau? Be patient; I shall not discuss ten, or even five. But we might in concluding our study achieve a greater concreteness, as well as entertain ourselves a little, by entering the minds of three such writers, two of an earlier period, one of a later; we might look out for a moment at the world of letters through the relatively naive eyes of Irving and Longfellow, and then through those of Henry James.

The overwhelming motivation of Irving's literary life, in relation to the patterns discussed, was *romance*. Gradually he came to feel the insecurity of the artist's life in America, and, far more of a scholar than is generally recognized, he loved the legendary material of Scott's library at Abbotsford, of Böttiger's in Dresden, or that of the antiquarian Johann Nikolaus Böhl von Faber in Puerto de Santa María. Yet such cosmopolitan values merely served, for him, a world of dreams and illusion, which, as he says in a beautiful letter written at the end of his life, alone made living precious: "Shadows have proved my substance; and from them I have derived many of my most exquisite enjoyments. . . . what fairy air castles of the mind I have built—*and inhabited.*"

Indeed, he was never a disciple of Addison and Goldsmith, as proclaimed in many a textbook, but rather a follower of Campbell, Byron, and Scott. The well-known phrases in his Introduction to *The Sketch Book* confirm the craving of his mind for romance: "I longed," he wrote, "to wander over the scenes of renowned achievement—to tread, as it were, in the footsteps of antiquity—to loiter about the ruined castle—to meditate on the falling tower—to escape, in short, from the [note his distressed recurrence to the word] commonplace realities of the present, and lose myself among the shadowy grandeurs of the past."

But ruined castles were few in New York or on the Hudson. He found no "shadowy grandeurs" when, at the age of nineteen, he was violently exposed to the mud and oxcarts of the Canadian frontier, or twenty-nine years later when in the Oklahoma blackjack he shot his bison and ate for his dinner in camp a skunk. He could not lose himself on the frontier, this born romantic, even in the checkered light of the rangers' campfire or in the brilliant colors of the Osage headdress. For he could do no better with such raw scenes than he had done in his early sketch of the Indian chief, "Philip of Pokanoket," in *The Sketch Book.* Trying to enter his mind, filled with stories heard from his English mother and from Walter Scott, we may disapprove, but we understand. Of course he must face toward Europe; of course he must write of Bracebridge Hall, and of the city of Granada, which, he says, "has ever been a subject of my waking dreams. How often have I trod in fancy the romantic halls of the Alhambra!"

If we repeat the experiment and next enter, so to speak, the cosmopolitan mind of Longfellow, the emphasis is suggestively different. Irving was interested in the books of Europe, was indeed steeped in a few—Shakespeare, Scott, Cervantes. Yet his vignettes of English, German, and Spanish peasants depended upon observation, as the Spanish novelist Fernán Caballero admiringly declared; he often described, with some accuracy, without the use of books, the ruined castle and the falling tower. On the other hand, Longfellow, a learned man, loved the books and repeated the tales therein almost without the aid of bodily presence at the ancient scenes.

Thus Longfellow spent only seven months in Spain in comparison with Irving's seven years; his garden of story and poem seemed to flower independently of his meager knowledge of the Peninsula. How beautifully he outlines in prose the heroic career of Don Jorge Manrique and how beautifully, too, he catches the spirit of the ancient chronicle in his opening lines from the *Coplas*:

> Oh let the soul her slumbers break,
> And thought be quickened, and awake;
> Awake to see
> How soon this life is past and gone,
> And death comes softly stealing on,
> How silently!

Then without the aid of direct knowledge, such as Irving's, of Andalusian peasant or Spanish nobleman, he gives us the strong,

untutored language of the ancient poem; he creates an image of
medieval manhood:

> By his unrivalled skill, by great
> And veteran service to the state,
> By worth adored,
> He stood, in his high dignity,
> The proudest knight of chivalry,
> Knight of the Sword.

Clearly Longfellow faced Europe, hardly glancing at the frontier, for the sake of its learning, its libraries, its languages, its
infinite wealth of bookish culture, of which ultimately he became
a master. It was Longfellow, not Irving, who thought Spain would
be valueless if, to use his own words, "the leaves were torn out
on which are written the names of Cervantes, Lope de Vega, and
Calderon." Irving could never have written of Spanish devotional
poetry or the Spanish language in the *North American Review*
any more than Longfellow could have created Irving's European
sketches. For Irving's aim, again quoting Fernán Caballero, who
worked with him hand in hand, was *poetizar la realidad.* Longfellow's aim, however, was to poetize what he found in European
books, without any reference to reality whatever. His incalcula-
ble service to his countrymen, starved for a Europe of which
they dreamed but which they could never visit, was to retell in
simple idiom the stories of this fabulous world. The cosmopolitan
Irving's mind was alive with European *scenes*; the cosmopolitan
Longfellow's with European *books.*

And so we might trace, one by one, the subtly different focuses
of the powerful influence of Europe upon different writers,
through the twenty, or thirty, or forty, from all of whom I merci-
fully spare you. I shall mention only one other, though he trans-
gresses my limit of time. If, in the main, the cosmopolitan Irving
faced Europe for its *places* and Longfellow for its *books,* Henry
James faced it (if we may describe as a voluntary act what
seems to have been congenital) for its society and the *mind* of
its society. James first knew European society not, like Hawthorne, at the age of fifty, not, like Longfellow, at the age of

twenty, but at the age of two. It was a regrettable delay! A portrait of the artist at the age of two seems unimportant, but James was always to remember from this early exposure (so ran the family tradition) the life about the Place Vendôme in Paris. At any rate, it was the first act. The second act reveals James as a boy in the Fourteenth Street house, surrounded by English books and Italian paintings. Once, in the next room, he heard the peculiar, throaty, cultivated voice of Washington Irving, back from Madrid: "I was," said James in later life of this period, "somehow in Europe, since everything about me had been 'brought over.'"

How predestined, how indigenous was this detachment from the American scene, this integration with the European! For James was not to care how men blow up a steamboat, as in Mark Twain; not how they perspire, as in Walt Whitman; not even about the falling tower, as in Irving, or about the medieval legend, as in Longfellow, but how civilized men and women think. In his pages is to be found a society in which the artist or writer can breathe, a society in which any man and woman grown in sensitivity beyond the stage of the American polyp can find life itself. That is, in these pages the reader lives on those levels of the mind and spirit which arise from conversation and silence, from unspoken friendships and unuttered hostilities, from faint ironies and remote adorations, from communions, shared or unshared with others, with music, painting, and sculpture.

In the leisure of this society meanings deepened and became equivocal; tensions in little things heightened; and all became symbol. A woman looked at you in a certain way, and the universe trembled slightly. What passed through the mind of Isabel Archer as she saw Madame Merle with Osmond—*seated?* In that of Christopher Newman as he heard the bronzed syllables of the Carmelites' bell? It was a strange and wonderful, if gossamer, world. James turned toward Europe to ensnare this elusive bird, as he called it; to solve this tenuous mystery of life, which wells from our deepest consciousness. Find the materials or moods for the creation of this world in America? Preposterous! He faced toward Europe.

In the first quotation from Henry James in this essay reference was made to "the negative side of the spectacle"—his phrase for the cultural sterility of America. We may now say, in all modesty, that the spectacle is no longer "negative." That about 1880 it became positive we owe in large measure to these cosmopolitans of the nineteenth century; in a sense, they were the true founders of our modern literary culture. Indeed, in our histories of literature I have always found irritating the allusions to "the genteel tradition," to the "anglophile literature," to the "European cult." I concede the absurdity of an entirely Europeanized literature, devoid of American subjects and American ideas. Yet I have never been able to agree with some of my colleagues that the era of Whitman, Mark Twain, and Joaquin Miller appeared as the only and the true Enlightenment. I have never felt that this vigorous era banished a kind of preliminary darkness. I have never believed that our cosmopolitan literature at its best is tainted with servility. I cannot, to paraphrase Shakespeare again, wish it undone, the issue of it being so proper—that is, so excellent. Although in this essay we have been chiefly concerned with causes, it is my hope that this paper has suggested also the brilliance of our cosmopolitan achievement in literature.

We prize them both, the shaggy giants of the frontier and the gentlemen-scholars in the capitals of Paris and Stockholm; the two urchins on a raft under the bright moonlight of the Mississippi, rolling its mile-wide tide along, and translations from Tegnér and Dante and also, I hope, though not without a little surprise that it is ours, such caviar as the following. Milly Theale had, the master cosmopolitan said, "arts and idiosyncracies of which no great account could have been given, but which were a daily grace if you lived with them; such as the art of being almost tragically impatient and yet making it as light as air; or being inexplicably sad and yet making it as clear as noon; of being unmistakably gay, and yet making it as soft as dusk." We

The American Writer and the European Tradition

must, I say, cherish in this literature of ours both the roughhewn and the esoteric. But, above all, we must not regard our cosmopolitan writing as a mere pronaos of books and artificiality to our literature of reality.

Indeed, to regard *The Wings of the Dove* and all the related patterns of our cosmopolitanism as merely an unfortunate phase of our adolescence seems to me essentially a criticism of the critic who so speaks. Learning and the love of literature lead inevitably to the founts of literature and learning: Irving at Abbotsford; Ticknor in Madrid; Longfellow at Uppsala; and Henry James on the *rive gauche*. These were inevitabilities which we cannot wish otherwise. Fear, emulation, confusion of purpose, sometimes harassed these founders of the cosmopolitan tradition in our literature, but deeply sincere was their belief that in their participation in these European regions of the mind lay for them spiritual fulfillment.

Origins of a Native American
Literary Tradition

OLIVER WENDELL HOLMES said that Emerson's address "The American Scholar" was our social and intellectual declaration of independence. The remark draws an analogy between politics and general culture that had long been a commonplace of American thought. In 1776 the colonies had enacted an ordinance of secession from Europe. They had made that ordinance good by war and had proceeded in 1787 to construct a political system for their nation that was entirely different from the monarchic systems of the Old World. Patriotic Americans considered their logical constitution far superior to the traditional and irrational political institutions they had left behind. Their government, they believed, was a product of reason not history. It offered an escape from the abuses and corruptions that Europe had inherited from a dark and evil past.

The United States thus began life with a strong general bias against tradition. Since the arts of Europe seemed to be organic parts of a decadent culture, American nationalism implied a certain hostility toward established patterns in art as well as in government. There was an excitement in the air derived from the belief that in the New World mankind could make a fresh start, could write the very first words upon a cultural *tabula rasa*. The utopian fantasies which were current in America during the latter part of the eighteenth century have a negative and anti-European tone. Crèvecœur, exulting in the belief that the society of the United States was the most nearly perfect then

63

existing in the world, specified that it contained "no aristocratic families, no courts, no kings, no bishops . . . no great manufacturers employing thousands . . . no great refinements of luxury"—and by implication no counterparts of the art galleries and court theaters of European capitals.[1]

But if the new nation rejected tradition as a guide to its development, what norms would it adopt? Toward what ruling ideas would it orient its literature and thought? Reason could be considered a sufficient guide in framing a system of government, but government was only a part, even though the most important part, of the nation's culture. The life of the imagination demanded a richer and more complex medium in which to develop. In their quest for a cultural ideal apart from tradition, Americans were led both by the dominant trends of eighteenth-century European thought and by their own geographical situation to turn to the fertile conception of nature. French and English thinkers had played a hundred variations upon the supposed antithesis between nature and civilization, and a well-developed theory of cultural primitivism held up nature as a norm capable of sustaining and underwriting all values, whether political, ethical, religious, or artistic. What could be more reasonable for men of the New World than to believe that in rejecting the civilization of Europe they were acting in the name of a pure and benevolent nature?

We must not of course imagine that the ideologists of revolution were able to control the intellectual life of the new nation or to convince all their countrymen that political independence logically implied cultural independence. Yet the ideas of the extreme left were formulated, they were set forth in print, and they provided, at least by implication, an esthetic creed for American society. Thomas Jefferson, listing "Objects of Attention for an American" as a guide for two of his countrymen about to set out for Europe in 1788, emphasized agriculture, mechanical arts, gardens, and architecture, but declared that painting and sculpture were "too expensive for the state of wealth among us." "It would be useless, therefore, and preposterous," he went on, "for us to make ourselves connoisseurs in those arts. They are worth seeing, but not studying."[2] An anonymous writer in Mathew Carey's *American Museum* in 1790 warned his fellow citizens against foreign luxuries and announced with philistine complacency that America must leave to posterity "the cultivation of the fine arts and the pleasures of taste and refinement."[3] Dr. Benjamin Rush explicitly urged American writers to free themselves from bondage to the decadent and artificial literature of England. "The present," he declared, "is the age of simplicity of writing in America. The turgid style of Johnson—the purple glare of Gibbon . . . should not be admitted into our country."[4]

Stated so baldly, this priggish view of the proper literary policy for a republic seems merely amusing. But there was a grain of truth in it. The American writer who tried to ignore the fact of the Revolution and to write as if he were a European found that literary modes were among the commodities which did not bear shipment across the Atlantic. Joseph Dennie, trying to conduct the *Port Folio* as if Philadelphia were the London of a former generation, became merely more shrill and more disgruntled with the passing years. American writers who actually tried (as Dennie did not) to deal with American experience found that their materials could not be adapted to English literary tradition. This incongruity between form and content, between imported convention and native experience, is evident at every level of artistic endeavor: not only in Daniel Bryan's Miltonic epic about Daniel Boone, which introduces councils in heaven and hell to prepare for the hero's struggle against the Cherokees in Kentucky, but in William Cullen Bryant's search for historical associations on the Illinois prairies and Washington Irving's discovery of rocks in Oklahoma resembling Moorish castles.

Cooper's Leatherstocking novels suffer from the same contradiction, for he was never able to move his admirably conceived backwoodsman up into the position of the technical hero of a conventional love story. Even Hawthorne felt baffled by the disparity between American experience and literary convention. "No author, without trial," he wrote in 1860, "can conceive of the difficulty of writing a romance about a country where there is no shadow, no antiquity, no mystery, no picturesque and gloomy wrong, nor anything but a commonplace prosperity, in broad and simple daylight, as is happily the case with my dear native land."[5] The measure of Hawthorne's greatness, and of Melville's, is that they were able to solve this problem for themselves by invoking the transcendental maxim that nature is the symbol of spirit and to create what fully deserves to be called personal forms of the novel. But these solutions were not available for the country as a whole because they presupposed two centuries of New England theological background.

Emerson, developing his doctrine of intuition into a cultural nationalism, emphatically rejected the notion of an American culture and literature developed as merely an adaptation of European tradition. The violence of his own reaction against the past in the sphere of theology gave to his teaching a somewhat doctrinaire flavor. He can be satirized as an insatiable reader denouncing books and a devotee of Plato declaring we have nothing to learn from the past. But he undoubtedly expressed something deeply felt and believed by his countrymen in his celebrated manifestoes of literary and cultural self-reliance. Since "The American Scholar" is so well known I shall illustrate Emerson's attitude by a less familiar entry in his journal:

We all lean on England; scarce a verse, a page, a newspaper, but is writ in imitation of English forms; our very manners and conversation are traditional, and sometimes the life seems dying out of all literature, and this enormous paper currency of Words is accepted instead.[6]

The remedy, which he had formulated for himself with so much pain and struggle, and which he commended to his countrymen with dogmatic assurance, was a reliance on nature.

As is often the case with dogmas, that of Emerson was open to a variety of interpretations. One reading of the oracle was that for the nation at large, nature meant the West. This notion had been implicit a half-century earlier in Tom Paine's declaration: ". . . there is something absurd, in supposing a continent to be

perpetually governed by an island."⁷ It had become national
policy with Jefferson's Louisiana Purchase and in the 1820s had
been elaborated into a rather pompous philosophy of the "continental" mission of the United States by Thomas Hart Benton.
In the 1840s, when the slogan of Manifest Destiny dominated
American thought, Emerson himself accepted the voice of the
people as a valid expression of his doctrine: ". . . the nervous,
rocky West is intruding a new and continental element into the
national mind, and we shall yet have an American genius."⁸ It
was this somewhat oratorical version of the doctrine of a culture
oriented toward the West that defined Whitman's vision of the
future of democratic America. "These States tend inland, and
toward the Western sea," he wrote, "and I will also."⁹ He sees
the corpse of tradition slowly borne from the house. The faded
kingdoms and kings of the Old World, the worn-out and weary
races of Europe yield precedence to stalwart American pioneers,
strong uncultivated persons with the continental blood inter-
vein'd. Even his passionate devotion to Lincoln owed a great
deal to the fact that Lincoln was a westerner without formal
education.

The line of development from Tom Paine to Whitman offers
abundant evidence that the implications of the American continental destiny were fully understood and that they commanded
widespread assent. If conceptual richness and logical consistency
can provide a basis for literature, then the relation of American
culture to its environment should have proved to be the dominant theme of nineteenth-century American literature. But of
course it was not. We have to look no further than Whitman
himself to perceive that a theory of this kind has no necessary
relation to actual literary achievement. Put together a selection
of Whitman's best poems and passages: "When Lilacs Last in
the Dooryard Bloom'd," "Out of the Cradle Endlessly Rocking,"
"Crossing Brooklyn Ferry," the good (as distinguished from the
bad) parts of "Song of Myself." These lines are not energized by
the theme of Manifest Destiny, and they are quite another thing
from the geographical catalogues or the rhetorical apostrophes

that Whitman wrote when he tried to do justice to his theory. It is not irrelevant to recall that despite Whitman's oratorical celebration of the West, he was one of the most determinedly urban of all our men of letters. The sea and the city are much more vivid symbols in his best work than are the prairies or the mountains of the West.

Yet the West did produce an important literature in the nineteenth century, and if it had little self-conscious nature-mysticism in it, it was certainly created without the support of European cultural tradition. This was the rough southwestern humor which reached literary fulfillment in Mark Twain. Here, too, Emerson had been prophetic, although his occasional insights did not lead him into a full analysis of the new thing that he saw appearing in the West. In the passage from the journal for 1834 that I have already quoted, after denouncing the American reliance upon England, Emerson goes on to remark:

I suppose the evil may be cured by this rank rabble party, the Jacksonism of the country, heedless of English and of all literature—a stone cut out of the ground without hands;—they may root out the hollow dilettantism of our cultivation in the coarsest way, and the newborn may begin again to frame their own world with greater advantage.[10]

Later, he expanded the theme in the *Dial*:

Our eyes will be turned westward, and a new and stronger tone in literature will be the result. The Kentucky stump-oratory, the exploits of Boon [*sic*] and David Crockett, the journals of western pioneers, agriculturalists, and socialists, and the letters of Jack Downing, are genuine growths, which are sought with avidity in Europe, where our European-like books are of no value.[11]

In acclaiming stump speeches and Davy Crockett's tall tales Emerson was being faithful to his intention of sitting at the feet of the familiar and low. The western reality that comes out in the barroom anecdotes and newspaper jokes, the comic almanacs and hunting yarns and painfully misspelled monologues of the humorous tradition bespeaks a society crude, raw, noisy, ugly, and vulgar: remote alike from Emerson's subtle doctrine of correspondence and from the chaste agrarian utopia painted in water colors by Crèvecœur and Jefferson. The people, as Whitman noted, perhaps without quite believing it himself, were gaunt and ungrammatical, and their sins were ill-bred. There was little of Platonism in the American Poet as he finally appeared in the guise of a southwestern lawyer or newspaper reporter writing squibs about coon-hunting, horse races, whiskey, and young people tumbling on the bed.

The character of this frontier humor is thoroughly familiar and I shall not go over such well-trodden ground. But I should like to make one distinction that is sometimes forgotten. The men who wrote the newspapers and almanacs must not be confused with the Davy Crocketts and Mike Finks and Sut Lovingoods they created. The frontier humor first got into print as sympathetic observation of primitive characters by men whose detachment and ability to record their amusement prove their relative sophistication. Walter Blair has traced the growth of this humorous mode to the influence of Walter Scott's portrayal of lowly types in Scotland. The framework device that is so common in the early sketches, with its introductory section setting the stage for the entrance of a backwoods character and its careful contrast between the correct and even elevated diction of the author and the dialect he puts into the mouths of his characters, clearly reflects the actual situation. It was not the Big Bear of Arkansas but the newspaper man from New Orleans who wrote the celebrated sketch for the *Spirit of the Times*.

What was primitive and unsophisticated about this southwestern humor was not the authors and their point of view but the materials. The attitude of a cultivated observer recording the quaint speech and manners of provincial characters was carried over into the local-color writing of the latter part of the century. The movement to use regional materials in fiction which gained momentum after the Civil War introduced a variety of themes and characters to American literature, and it served a sociological function by acquainting a national audience with the peculiarities of the various sections of the country. But local-color fiction is negligible, on the whole, as art. The most important contribution of western humor lay in a different direction, in the development effected by Mark Twain when he abandoned the framework device altogether to write *Huckleberry Finn* from the point of view and in the language of a half-literate small-town boy. This choice of method not only enabled Mark Twain to write his greatest book—perhaps his only really great one—but transmitted to the twentieth century certain highly important conceptions of the nature of American prose. An examination of Mark Twain's work therefore offers the best means of getting at what happened when American writers turned their backs on Europe.

In reading Mark Twain's early books we discover at once that if the westerner turned away from Europe, he frequently felt the impulse to look over his shoulder. He understood perfectly that Europe had a monopoly of traditional culture, and that he was undertaking an audacious experiment when he proposed to get along without the aid of tradition. The repudiation of Europe is a different thing from indifference to it.

The most obvious, perhaps the inevitable, attitude which a westerner would take up when he confronted the momentous phenomenon of the Old World was that of an ignoramus, a barbarian—or, as Mark Twain himself accurately puts it, an innocent. But these are ambiguous terms. Barbarism implies ignorance and crudity and lack of ethical discipline. Yet it also has its positive aspect: the barbarian can conceive of himself according to the time-honored conception of the Noble Savage, the man who lacks the vices as well as the virtues of civilization, and who has an innate integrity based upon communion with nature. From the earliest discovery of America, a long succession of writers both in Europe and later in this country had conceived of Americans in general after this fashion; and with the increasing social maturity of the Eastern Seaboard of the United States, the attributes of the Noble Savage had been ascribed to westerners. Mark Twain alludes to this set of attitudes when he classes himself as an innocent.

The critique of Europe (or, if you like, of the exaggerated veneration for Europe which Mark Twain detected in his fellow countrymen) that is set forth in *Innocents Abroad* is not merely negative, not merely a destructive burlesque. It is built upon an affirmation. The Americans, including the author's imaginative projection of himself, stand for purity, for naiveté, for progress and democracy and the future. The Europe against which they array themselves is not merely acres of Rubenses, but the past in general: monarchy, poverty, illiteracy, dirt, and perhaps most of all, the Church, which stands as the embodiment of all these aspects of the historic past. In other words, Mark Twain's social judgments tend again and again toward the general position of eighteenth-century radicalism. Minnie Brashear has demonstrated that these ideas were current in the Missouri of Mark Twain's youth, where they had been conveyed through the instrumentality of Tom Paine's works. Church and throne—these are the twin evils that the unsophisticated westerner can see at the root of everything that disgusts him in Europe. His emphasis is political. His awareness of social wrongs is so vivid that the problem of whether the art of the Old World may actually embody a value inaccessible to him becomes irrelevant. Mark Twain was willing to forgive Louis XIV for his tyranny when he saw the gardens of Versailles, but this was a passing mood and he returned more often to indignation like that he felt in Rome when he contrasted the gorgeous marble of St. Peter's with the wretchedness of the common people who filled the slums of the city.

This repudiation of Europe, which runs like a thread through many books, has neither more nor less bearing upon literature than does Whitman's creed of Manifest Destiny. Both sets of ideas are simply raw materials which the writer may or may not be able to transform into art. I have already ventured the opinion that Whitman's expansionism did not nourish his best poetry. I am tempted to say the same of Mark Twain's use of the heritage of eighteenth-century radicalism. *A Connecticut Yankee*, the work in which these ideas are most prominent, is far from representing his highest imaginative level. Nevertheless, there are some passages that show what happens when such an abstract set of doctrines is stated in metaphorical and symbolic terms. Since I wish to have an example of Mark Twain's work before us in order to comment on his literary method, I shall quote a passage in which political ideas have been transmuted into art.

The Yankee relates that when he goes with the Lady Alisaunde (or Sandy) on a knightly mission to free a number of beautiful and noble ladies from a dire enchantment, he finds what appears to him to be a drove of hogs. Sandy, on the other hand, perceives these hogs as her friends, transformed by the black arts of the necromancer. So much of the incident is no doubt borrowed from *Don Quixote.* But from this point onward we are caught up into the mode of the tall tale. There is a new and authentic act of the imagination in Hank's straight-faced account of his difficulties with the bewitched princesses:

The troublesomest old sow of the lot had to be called my Lady, and your Highness, like the rest . . . There was one small countess, with an iron ring in her snout and hardly any hair on her back, that was the devil for perversity. She gave me a race of an hour, over all sorts of country, and then we were right where we had started from, having made not a rod of real progress. I seized her at last by the tail, and brought her along squealing. When I overtook Sandy she was horrified, and said it was in the last degree indelicate to drag a countess by her train.

It is possible, although not certain, that one of the sources of interest in this passage is its metaphorical introduction of the whole theme of the book, the Yankee's determination to hurry forward social progress in Arthur's England against the opposition of the nobility. In any event, the main intention of degrading feudal aristocracy is developed to the limit in the rest of the passage:

The princess Nerovens de Morganore was missing, and two of her ladies in waiting: namely, Miss Angela Bohun, and the Demoiselle Elaine Courtemains, the former of these two being a young black sow with a white star in her forehead, and the latter

a brown one with thin legs and a slight limp in the forward
shank on the starboard side . . .[12]

This is small in scale, but it illustrates how the American repudiation of Europe could be expressed in the western literary
mode. The technical precision of a county-seat newspaper ad-
vertisement for lost stock is set in tension against the wild
fantasy of the situation. The result is a species of poetic irony.
Such writing does not come by accident. It is the end product
of a long-continued, workmanlike preoccupation with the basic
literary strategy of Mark Twain's predecessors in frontier humor.
The root of the matter is the creation of a certain type of sensibility: the point of view of an illiterate yet entirely self-possessed
observer and critic, learned in the ways of hogs but without
social pretensions, external to and hostile toward upper-class
institutions. His apparent humility masks a deep purity and a
disconcerting poise. He has, in fact, the traits that William
Empson has taught us to see in the shepherd of pastoral tradition. Mark Twain's best work results from an exhaustive exploration of such an observed and imagined sensibility.

One of the most important literary consequences of this fixa-
tion upon the uncultivated backwoodsman was the discovery of
the richness of vernacular speech. The systematic misspellings
of Artemus Ward and Josh Billings were a misguided tribute to
the felt imaginative significance of the vernacular, but its real
power lay elsewhere, in the stock of metaphorical material at its
disposal, its oral rhythms, its diction at once elaborate and able
to put the reader at ease by making no demands upon formal
culture. The vernacular was exploited first for comic purposes,
and Mark Twain began with a mastery of these possibilities—
as in the chapter "Scotty Briggs and the Parson" in *Roughing It.*
But a comic mode, especially this rather innocent one, is limited
in scope. Not until he reshaped the vernacular to serve the whole
range of demands that a novelist might make on language did
Mark Twain show his full mastery of the medium.

For an example let us take the theme of man's communion

with nature. In the Romantic poets this theme had seemed to demand the loftiest diction. But in *Huckleberry Finn* Mark Twain phrases some of the most intense nature poetry in our literature in an effortless vernacular idiom:

Here is the way we put in the time. It was a monstrous big river down there—sometimes a mile and a half wide; we run nights, and laid up and hid daytimes; soon as night was most gone we stopped navigating and tied up—nearly always in the dead water under a towhead; and then cut young cottonwoods and willows, and hid the raft with them. Then we set out the lines. Next we slid into the river and had a swim, so as to freshen up and cool off; then we set down on the sandy bottom where the water was about knee-deep, and watched the daylight come. Not a sound anywheres—perfectly still—just like the whole world was asleep, only sometimes the bullfrogs a-cluttering, maybe. The first thing to see, looking away over the water, was a kind of dull line— that was the woods on t'other side; you couldn't make nothing else out; then a pale place in the sky; then more paleness spreading around; then the river softened up away off, and warn't black any more, but gray; you could see little dark spots drifting along ever so far away—trading-scows, and such things; and long black streaks—rafts; sometimes you could hear a sweep screaking; or jumbled-up voices, it was so still, and sounds come so far; and by and by you could see a streak on the water which you know by the look of the streak there's a snag there in a swift current which breaks on it and makes that streak look that way; and you see the mist curl up off of the water, and the east reddens up, and the river, and you make out a log cabin in the edge of the woods, away on the bank on t'other side of the river, being a wood-yard, likely . . .

The syntax of this description, its easy succession of "and's" and "then's," is as important as the diction in developing the mood of absolute relaxation. The experience is rendered with precision at the level of sense-perception but has T. S. Eliot's unconscious generality. What is most interesting about the passage, perhaps, is the way in which Mark Twain deliberately controls the incipient sentimentality of the mood of communion with nature by an ironic deflation of it. The conclusion uses the familiar device of anticlimax:

. . . being a wood-yard, likely, and piled by them cheats so you can throw a dog through it anywheres; then the nice breeze springs up, and comes fanning you from over there, so cool and fresh and sweet to smell on account of the woods and the flowers; but sometimes not that way, because they've left dead fish laying around, gars and such, and they do get pretty rank; and next you've got the full day, and everything smiling in the sun, and the song-birds just going it![13]

Without invoking an elaborate philosophy, this description perfectly establishes Huck's and Jim's closeness to nature and contrasts this peace with the ugliness that human society brings into the virgin world of the river. The contrivance is entirely conscious, the loosely stacked wood and the gars most of all, for the passage introduces the chapter in which the rascally Duke and King first come aboard the raft.

These are some of the effects to which the western humorous mode could be brought. At their best they are very good indeed, fully able to stand beside the widely different triumphs of *The Scarlet Letter* and *Moby Dick*. But there was a price to be paid for the freedom and freshness American writers could attain when they cut themselves loose from literary tradition. For one thing, backwoods humor was of little help in solving the architectural problems of the novel. It provided an abundance of characters and incidents, a prose of rich texture, a literary strategy with fertile possibilities of variation, but it developed no tradition of major form. *Huckleberry Finn* is a series of anecdotes rather than an organized work of art. The voyage down the river gives it narrative shape of a sort, but the theme of Jim's escape to freedom up the Ohio does not harmonize with the steady southward sweep of the current of the Mississippi and is eventually abandoned. The moral crisis in which Huck decides to help Jim escape even though this means defying all the mores of his society, with its climax in his superb exclamation, "All right, then, I'll *go* to hell!" is grievously undercut by Mark Twain's subsequent revelation that Jim had already been freed in Miss Watson's will. The effort to supply a plot by introducing the complications surrounding Peter Wilks' will is a feeble borrowing from the melodramatic stage. And the long extravaganza at the end, when we are invited to enjoy a hundred pages of Tom Sawyer's rigmarole of rescuing Jim, is a source of discomfort to every reader.

As these final chapters suggest, moreover, the western tradition had not developed canons of taste to replace the ones it had abandoned. Mark Twain is an unreliable writer. He seems unable to distinguish between his best pages and his worst. Long after he wrote *Huckleberry Finn* he was capable of building two novelettes around the theme of Siamese twins. Even in his greatest book he can lose himself in a parody of Hamlet's soliloquy and can ask us to believe that the camp-meeting crowd is taken in by the King's tale of being a pirate from the Indian Ocean. It is equally important to realize that the western tradition was intellectually naive. It could not deal with ideas in any profound or creative fashion. The abstract conceptions that Mark Twain had derived from the Enlightenment had become thin and shopworn indeed by the end of the nineteenth century. The philosophy of determinism, for example, which he elaborated with so much effort and viewed with so much awe, is a restatement of ideas that were commonplaces to thinkers like Helvetius and are simple-minded even in the eighteenth-century versions which were Mark Twain's ultimate sources.

And yet American literature of the twentieth century owes a substantial debt to the author of *Huckleberry Finn*. Writers as different from one another as Sherwood Anderson and Ernest Hemingway have acknowledged the influence of this book on their prose, and in addition one has to take into account the development of the humorous mode by writers like E. B. White, James Thurber, S. J. Perelman, and A. J. Liebling. These evidences demonstrate an important continuity in literary technique and attitude. Where the followers of Whitman have too often moved toward the loose oratory of Thomas Wolfe or Carl Sandburg, the influence of Mark Twain has encouraged discipline and craftsmanship. Paradoxically enough, the rank rabble party of Jacksonism turns out to have set in motion an austere cult of style that has given to American literature an esthetic tradition as pure and rigorous as that of the Symbolists themselves.

Notes

[1] *Letters from an American Farmer* (London: Thomas Davies and Lockyer Davies, 1782) 46–48.

[2] *Writings,* Monticello edition (Washington: Thomas Jefferson Memorial Association, 1904) XVII, 292.

[3] *American Museum,* vol. 7, p. 240 (May).

[4] *Ibid.,* vol. 4, p. 443 (November 1788).

[5] Preface to *The Marble Faun* (Boston: Houghton, Mifflin, 1888) 15.

[6] *Journals,* ed. Edward Waldo Emerson and Waldo Emerson Forbes (Boston: Houghton, Mifflin, 1883–1914) III, 308, June 18, 1834.

[7] *Political Writings* (New York: Solomon King, 1830) I, 40.

[8] "The Young American," in *Nature, Addresses, and Lectures* (Boston: Houghton, Mifflin, 1904) 370.

[9] *Leaves of Grass* (Boston: Thayer and Eldridge, 1860) 371.

[10] *Journals,* III, 308.

[11] *Dial,* vol. 3, pp. 511–12 (April 1843).

[12] *A Connecticut Yankee in King Arthur's Court* (New York: Harper, n.d.) 175–76 (Chapter XX).

[13] *The Adventures of Huckleberry Finn* (New York: Harper, n.d.) 163–64 (Chapter XIX).

❧ LEON HOWARD ❧

Americanization of the European Heritage

THE young men of letters who reached their maturity in early nineteenth-century America were in a rather peculiar situation. They were heirs to a great literary tradition which was, by virtue of their language and education, as truly their own as it would have been had they been born in England. Yet they were obliged to claim their heritage in surroundings quite different from those in which it had been developed, in a country which was already beginning to turn its back on Europe and develop a distinctive tradition of its own. The American tradition did not yet have within itself the creative force necessary to produce a great piece of original literature, but it did have the power to make the literature of England seem foreign and somewhat out of place on the western side of the Atlantic. Most of the men who succeeded in achieving permanent literary fame, accordingly, were those who succeeded in adapting the English— or, in some cases, European—tradition to American needs and thus producing a literature which naturalized the European intellect in an American environment. The most vigorous early examples of American literature, in short, were the fruit of grafting foreign ideas and literary interests upon characteristically native ways of thinking.

Such a generalization in figurative language is vague enough to be accepted as a commonplace. Whether it is useful in providing any new insight into the American past as preserved in the country's literature depends entirely upon whether such terms as the European heritage and the American tradition can be translated into perceptible realities and whether the process of "naturalization" or "grafting" can be described in plain terms and illustrated by specific examples.

The European heritage offers no particular difficulties. It consisted in the first half of the nineteenth century of a body of literary material—ranging from the rationalism of the French philosophers to the transcendentalism of the Germans and from the grotesque fancies of the Gothic romance to the solid realities of scientific investigation—which had come into existence in Europe and had then crossed the Atlantic to provide some of the substance of literature in America.

The American tradition is more tenuous. Its distinctive quality may be observed in the homely wisdom of Benjamin Franklin or in his shrewd use of a plain garb for the purpose of making an impression upon the elegant court of Louis XVI. It may be found in the ingrained consciousness of everyday realities which made Americans take delight in flights of fancy, either in oratory or in the tall tales of the frontier, while priding themselves on their refusal to be taken in by the exhibitions they enjoyed. It is a tradition exemplified in an attitude of mind that has never been properly described in a single adjective, although such terms as hard-headed, realistic, and pragmatic have been applied to it. The process of naturalizing the European heritage or grafting it upon the American tradition was one of adapting such literary material to this pragmatic attitude of mind and thus making it appeal to American readers by giving it what Europeans might call an American stamp or character. The result was something like what Nathaniel Hawthorne called "wisdom that had been tested by the tenor of a life" or, in more colloquial language, something that made sense in terms of one's individual experience. The attempt to take European literary material and test it by the tenor of their own lives—to change it into something that made sense in terms of their own experience—is the distinctive American characteristic, I believe, which can be found in such writers as Emerson and Thoreau, Hawthorne, Herman Melville, Edgar Allan Poe, and Walt Whitman. It may also be the characteristic which gave them the vitality they seem to have preserved to a greater degree than any other American writers before the Civil War.

The first illustrations of this process may be found in Emerson, whose little book published in 1836, *Nature,* dealt with two apparently contradictory lines of literary interest which were strong in England at that time. The earlier of these was the romantic interest in nature which had characterized English poetry and much English prose for a generation—the sort of devotion which caused Wordsworth to call nature the anchor of his purest thoughts and the soul of all his moral being, which Coleridge mourned as something he had lost in turning to the abstruse researches of philosophy, and in which Byron professed to find refreshment for his world-weariness. The later was an enthusiasm for the new transcendental philosophy which first Coleridge and then Carlyle had imported from Germany and spread abroad in England and in America, where Carlyle was better known than he was in his own country. This new philosophy placed a great stress upon the value of absolute Reason (which may be very roughly defined as intuitive perception) as a means of knowing and, in Carlyle's version of it at least, vigorously emphasized the superior importance of the immaterial world of the spirit to the physical world of matter. The physical world in fact, according to Carlyle's *Sartor Resartus,* existed only for the purpose of symbolizing the real world of the spirit and thus to "body it forth" to the understanding of men whose inner eyes were blind.

The romantic, whole-hearted devotion to Alps and daffodils and the transcendental indifference to them as anything other than symbols of some spiritual reality were theoretically incompatible: one could not be, logically, a genuine nature-lover and also a devotee of transcendental philosophy as preached by Carlyle. Yet Emerson was. He revealed his sensuous delight in the physical world through the imagery of his verse and freely professed it in his essays, and he found his greatest intellectual stimulation in the transcendental philosophy. When he tested the wisdom of Carlyle by the tenor of his own life—when he tried to find in his own "condition," as he expressed it, "a solution in hieroglyphic to those inquiries he would put"—he discovered that this wisdom did not, in its original state, make perfect sense. He could not dismiss physical nature as nothing more than "a garment of the Spirit." The result was that his little book exemplified a new kind of transcendentalism, a transcendentalism with at least one foot on the ground, which compromised with everyday realities and even attempted to justify the "noble doubt" of philosophical idealism by arguments from common experience. It is not very impressive philosophically, perhaps, but Emerson's great literary appeal has been the result of his ability to unite— a European might say "confuse"—the refined philosophical doctrines of transcendentalism with the common thoughts and impulses of ordinary people so successfully that there seem to be no significant differences between them.

But Emerson, despite his Yankee ability to turn Olympus into a huckleberry hill, was an extraordinarily high-minded man who persistently tried to abstract the thoughts of his readers and hearers from their everyday lives. The thoroughly naturalized character of the new American brand of transcendentalism can only be seen in the practical expression of Emerson's theories by his young friend and hard-headed disciple Henry David Thoreau. The author of *Walden* did not worry, as Emerson did in *Nature*, about why the physical world existed or whether it was real. He accepted it without hesitation as the most delightful actuality of his life and indulged his delight without feeling that he was violating those "higher laws" which governed his transcendental being. Examining his own "condition," he found within himself "an instinct toward a higher, or, as it is named, spiritual life" and also "another toward a primitive rank and savage one." He reverenced them both, deriving mental and spiritual inspiration from the sensuous taste of a berry and apparently taking a sardonic satisfaction in the fact that it seemed impossible to draw any practical distinction between the currents of universal Being and the circulating sap of a bush.

He recognized two selves on which he could rely—the inner,

spiritual self, about which Emerson had talked as a part of the divine spirit or Oversoul; and an outer, physical self which could subsist upon beans and thus achieve simplicity amid the complexities of the everyday world. Their relationship was not one of contradictions nor was it the relationship of reality and emblem. They were complementary and could be merged into a single whole. For Thoreau had learned from his experiment at Walden Pond that in proportion as a man "simplifies his life, the laws of the universe will appear less complex, and solitude will not be solitude, nor poverty poverty, nor weakness weakness."

Thoreau's practical transcendentalism not only succeeded in reconciling a love of nature with a devotion to the spirit but it reconciled them in such a way that freedom of the spirit was achieved through a practical intimacy with nature. Because of this common-sensible independence which was characteristic of the native literary tradition, an ordinary American could indulge in transcendental inclinations without feeling the compulsion toward the hero worship advocated by Carlyle. When it got both feet on the ground the new philosophy had been naturalized and had become democratic in its western environment.

While the transcendentalists were engaged in grafting one body of European ideas upon the native stock of pragmatic realism Nathaniel Hawthorne was engaged in a similar enterprise with a different literary tradition. For Hawthorne, in cultivating the art of fiction, had made himself a follower of Scott and the Gothic romancers although he dwelt upon the New England past and used its store of legendary superstitions. His stories, however, soon became something more than specimens of American Gothic. The quality of his intellect was observant and boldly inductive; and as he looked at life and collected instances of human behavior, his romances became moral parables which made sense in terms of his own observation, however unconventional they might be in their conclusions.

The earliest of his short stories and the first of his mature novels each told the story of a woman who had committed adultery, but in the two decades that intervened between them he learned enough to change the moral of his story from "the wages of sin is death" to a suggestion that the result of sin may be either a strengthening or a destruction of character, depending upon whether the individual openly accepts the social consequences of his action or broods upon them in secret. In his hands the Gothic romance and historical novel changed from a tale of terror and a narrative of colorful excitement into a psychological study which was as realistic in its observations upon the inner lives of its characters as it was romantic or artificial in its representation of their external appearances. Just as Thoreau, in his individual way, united nature and spirit in a manner which led to the creation of something new and characteristically American, so Hawthorne, after his fashion, combined romantic fantasy with psychological realism and created something equally new and equally characteristic. The same quality of hard-headed dependence upon personal experience rather than upon theory may be seen in both.

It may be seen from even these few illustrations that the down-to-earth quality of the American tradition was reflected in literature in different ways. Among the major transcendentalists it operated as a practical restraint upon high-flying intellects, keeping their philosophy from carrying them off above the clouds. With Hawthorne, its operation was intellectual, anchoring his flights of romantic fancy to the firm reality of his observations upon life and human nature. Occasionally when these two contrasting attitudes of mind, the intuitionalism of the transcendentalists and the inductive reasoning of Hawthorne, came into conflict in the work of a single American author they gave an unusual energy of intellectual strife to his major work.

Such an author was Herman Melville. In his early works he had no trouble reconciling his practical observations with an unreasoned belief in the inherent goodness of unspoiled human nature. What he had seen of civilization as a young man in a period of financial depression had been deeply discouraging. What he saw of the primitivistic state of nature among the savages of the South Sea islands was relatively delightful. And when

he wrote, in such books as *Typee* and *Omoo,* of the evil results
of the westward march of civilization, he expressed opinions that
might have been reached by either romantic theorizing or inductive reasoning. But as he grew in mind and in knowledge and as
the range of his intellectual theorizing increased, he became involved in a conflict between the romantic will to believe and the
realistic demand to be shown. It was this conflict—actually between a heritage of European philosophy and a characteristically
American attitude of mind—that moved him to his most powerful expression in prose.

For Captain Ahab, the hero of *Moby Dick,* was such a mad-
man as Emerson might have understood, although Melville inter-
preted him in such a manner as Hawthorne might have used. He
was in fact apparently intended to be a sort of seagoing version
of Carlyle's Teufelsdröckh, who had been caught for characteri-
zation in the defiance of his "Everlasting No"—at a time when
he saw physical objects as emblematic masks for some spiritual
reality but before he achieved his optimistic belief that the universe was not a machine designed for his destruction. Melville
condemned him, as Hawthorne would have done, as a mono-
maniac, attributed his tragic fate to his monomania, and analyzed
his disease in terms like those applied to Arthur Dimmesdale in
The Scarlet Letter. But the flat condemnation did not come
easily to Melville. It violated his earlier observations which attributed the evils of the world to the environmental influences
of civilization rather than to the inner impulses of the individual;
and it contradicted his later book *Pierre* in which he probed, with
every evidence of open-mindedness, the question of whether the
transcendental impulse was a trustworthy guide to be followed
or whether it was the sort of "lying spirit" which had sent Ahab
of old and Ahab anew to his bad end.

The vigor and life of *Moby Dick* did not come from the teaching of its fable or from the rhetoric in which it was presented but
from the intellectual tension developed when Melville tried to
put an emotionally attractive philosophy to the test of a personal experience which had not yet resulted in settled convic-

tions. The will to believe was strong in him but the demand to be shown could not be resisted. He could not, like Thoreau, reverence both sides of his nature alike. He felt obliged to choose between them. But he could not readily lean, with Emerson, toward one or, with Hawthorne, toward the other. In a sense, *Moby Dick* and *Pierre* each represent the failure of an author to unite his European and his American heritage, but the effort to do so produced two of the most stimulating books in nineteenth-century literature.

The importance of the distinctively American tradition, even to an author who completely failed to use it, may be seen in the case of Edgar Allan Poe. For Poe occupied a peculiar position among American authors. Reared as an orphan in a city of self-conscious sons and grandsons, trained to live the life of a gentleman with the financial resources of a beggar, and condemned to call himself a Bostonian in an accent from Virginia, he was a socially displaced person. In a country which demanded that a man should keep his feet on the ground, Poe had no solid ground on which to stand—no secure tenor of life by which he could test his heritage of European literary influences and transform them into something entirely his own. When Poe tried to use his romantic heritage from Europe, he succeeded, instead of absorbing it as Hawthorne did, merely in losing himself in it, taking on the personality of Byron or Coleridge or occasionally Keats, Shelley, and De Quincey. He was not, like Byron, playing a romantic role of his own creation but rather was playing a role created for him abroad. Eventually these personalities combined to form the composite hero of "The Raven," who united the characteristics of Childe Harold with those of the author of the "Ode to Dejection"—a pale and interesting character who was exiled from the world by his own dark mind and spent his time in an effort to deaden his imagination and his afflictions by abstruse research in strange and curious volumes of forgotten lore. To many casual readers, to the French followers of Baudelaire, and to some American biographers, that was the true Poe.

But it was not the whole truth to the man himself. He felt a strong need for a firmly matter-of-fact personality such as Hawthorne, for example, really possessed; and, lacking a background into which he could settle, he created it as a complement to the romantic role he had adopted. The result was the hard-boiled book reviewer, the solver of cryptograms, the predecessor of Sherlock Holmes, and the would-be philosopher who attempted to solve the riddle of the universe in *Eureka*. He placed his second personality before the public as his real one when he wrote "The Philosophy of Composition" and claimed that he worked out "The Raven" as a problem in emotional engineering, calculating his effects and nicely selecting the means by which he would achieve them. His creation is no more real than his adoption, but the fact that Poe seems to have found it necessary to develop a second personality bears witness to the American impulse to keep one's feet on the ground even when there was no solid ground available for them to stand on.

It is a curious fact that the successful union of European literary interests and an American state of mind is more evident in the native prose of the first half of the nineteenth century than in verse. Although William Cullen Bryant was a determined and Joseph Rodman Drake an enthusiastic advocate of the use of American materials, among the early poets, neither was peculiarly American in his characteristic approach to them. Longfellow, too, seems to have approached his American materials from a personally detached if not a European point of view; and the work of Whittier and Lowell which at first glance seems most indigenous was directed by the spirit of Bobby Burns, either in its attempt to glorify common things and common people or in its use of rustic dialect. The first number of Lowell's *Biglow Papers*, it is true, succeeded in translating some of the political generalizations of the time into the homely realism of a down-to-earth character; but Hosea Biglow lost his personality as the series progressed and became nothing more than an apologist for Lowell's changes of opinion, although he retained his Yankee shrewdness as a characterizing humor. Poe kept his poetry in his romantic dream world, and even Emerson, whose literary character was unusually consistent, cut loose his moorings and rose to transcendental heights in verse that he never dared in his most inspired prose. These writers appear to have made a distinction between man and poet and to have felt that they had not only a poetic license but almost an obligation to ignore the controlling restraint of individual experience.

Walt Whitman, however, was an exception who literally identified the poet with the man and achieved his greatest originality by adapting the generalities of European philosophy to the particular earthiness of his individual self. A substantial measure of the impetus which launched Whitman on his mature career may, in fact, have come from the traditional theory which identified a poem with the individuality of its author and led to the notion that a work of literature should grow naturally out of its creator rather than be an object of calculated design. Whitman preached that doctrine constantly and, with the curious literal-mindedness of the half-educated, celebrated precisely those qualities in his verse which had been discovered in him by a phrenological analysis—love of comrades, benevolence, expansiveness, and self-esteem, which were found to be his outstanding virtues, and sensuousness and recklessness, which were considered his faults. Yet the "self" of Whitman's verse was more than that of the individual poet so clearly revealed in the analysis of the "chart of bumps" he had bound into the first edition of *Leaves of Grass*. It was even more than a representative of the "average man" of nineteenth-century America who participated in all the activities and occupied all the stations of life that Whitman catalogued with such avidity in his works. It was something between a reality and a symbol representing Whitman's effort to test the wisdom of philosophy "by the tenor of a life."

The two major lines of European thought which Whitman naturalized in the early editions of *Leaves of Grass* were, first, the eighteenth-century rationalism which he derived from his early reading of Volney, Tom Paine, and Elias Hicks and, second, the early scientific theories of evolution which had developed in conjunction with the work of the French zoologist Lamarck and the English geologists James Hutton and Sir Charles Lyell. The rationalists had taught him that humankind had been corrupted by civilization, that the ideal state was a state of nature, and that the religion of humanity needed no priesthood. Whitman took their abstract doctrines and individualized them by translating them into his own personality, making his real self a symbol of the natural man who loafed and invited his soul or took to the open road, sounding his barbaric yawp over the roof of the world and re-examining philosophies and religions to see whether they would prove themselves as well under the spacious clouds as they did in lecture rooms. Much of his literary achievement is the result of his success in taking a philosophy which the eighteenth century had found inspiring in the intellectual language peculiar to that age and translating it into a form of expression which communicated the inspiration to another generation.

He tried to do the same thing with more modern scientific theories, finding in his extraordinary "self" man as a species— the acme of things accomplished in the evolutionary process and the encloser of things to be, who had evolved from original Nothing through eras of fetid carbon and monstrous sauroids until he stood with his robust soul in full confidence of the future. The symbolism of the individual as the representative of a stage in the evolutionary process is successful enough in the "Song of Myself," but the personal experience of evolving, of course, is not there; and Whitman's effort to incorporate modern science into his verse was, on the whole, better expressed in his declarations of intention than revealed in his accomplishment. Nevertheless, Whitman illustrates, perhaps better than anyone else, that distinctive effort to adjust European ideas to the tenor of individual life which was characteristic of the most successful makers of American literature during this period.

In so far as these illustrations make sense—in terms of one's own observations, of course—it is possible to speak of the naturalization of European ideas and the grafting of foreign material upon native ways of thinking in a way that will lead to a better understanding of the peculiarly American quality of

American literature. It was not a quality which estranged the American writer completely from his English cousin, however, for it is a reflection of that characteristic which has made Englishmen successful colonists and English colonies incorrigibly independent. English writers have naturally shared it. Yet if Emerson is compared with Carlyle, Hawthorne with William Godwin or George Eliot, or Whitman with Robert Browning, the English authors appear noticeably more inclined toward the Continental tendency to ask that their experience make sense in terms of some ideology. The literature of America lacks the formal intellectual quality which so consistently characterizes that of Europe and, to a lesser degree, that of England; but it does not lack an individual intellectual vigor which comes from the attempt to reduce an accepted doctrine to a personal belief. It is this unconventional flavor of individualism which keeps these literary fruits of American ingenuity—to the taste of some people, at least—fresh.

American Writers
as Critics of Nineteenth-Century Society

EMERSON was forty-eight when he first spoke passionately about American affairs. The date was May 3, 1851, and the occasion his address on the Fugitive Slave Law before his fellow citizens of Concord. The idol of New England, Daniel Webster, had crashed to the ground on the seventh of March 1850 when he put the preservation of the Union above the abolition of slavery. Emerson was at last aroused by this defection and his denunciation of Webster and his kind cuts like an edged knife. He came over to the side of the doers.

He had, of course, spoken about the issues of American life since his appearance before the American Peace Society in 1838 with his theoretical address on "War." Many of his friends were reformers and they had not ceased to urge their causes on him. But Emerson had preserved a certain detachment and aloofness all these years, caused, among other circumstances, by a fundamental bias in his nature, of which I shall speak in a moment. His early addresses on public affairs are in the main theoretical. They invariably call for the reform of the individual. They do not advocate causes. Even as late as 1840 he writes resentfully in his *Journal* of the way he permits himself to be diverted: "I have not yet conquered my own house. It irks and repents me. Shall I raise the siege of this hencoop, and march baffled away to a pretended siege of Babylon? It seems to me that so to do were to dodge the problem I am set to solve, and to hide my impotency in the thick of a crowd."

Though he occasionally did what the reformers asked of him,

he was skeptical of any good which might result. Thus, in 1838, he was persuaded to draft a letter to President Van Buren on the occasion of the forced removal of the Cherokees from Georgia to the trans-Mississippi region. The letter is eloquent enough, but Emerson noted in his *Journal*:

Yesterday went the letter to Van Buren, a letter hated of me, a deliverance that does not deliver the soul . . . This stirring in the philanthropic mud gives me no peace. I will let the Republic alone until the Republic comes to me. I fully sympathize, to be sure, with the sentiment I write, but I accept it rather from my friends than dictate it. It is not my impulse to say it, and therefore my genius deserts me. No muse befriends, no music of thought or word accompanies. Bah!

Remembering the Emerson who eventually became the spokesman for radical America, we are likely to forget the young Emerson and his struggle to formulate what he early called the "first philosophy." His task was a mighty one. He had to justify the break with his Unitarian heritage, which had already brought him, before he was thirty, a measure of fame. He had to think his way to a new religion which would have the strength of Puritanism, but would be affirmative, joyous, and practical where Puritanism had been negative and gloomy, a faith impossible for men to live by. And this new religion, to be complete, must satisfy the young idealist's explorations in the ethical, scientific, and esthetic realms. To follow Emerson in his quest, as he records his tentative conclusions in his journals, is a most exciting adventure for any student of American thought. The culminating point is 1836 when he published *Nature*. It is significant that though the pages of the journals permit you to follow his trail right into the chapters of *Nature*, there are during these years very few entries having to do with political or economic affairs. It was not until two years later that he made his first important speech on a public issue—the address on "War." He seems to have kept his mind deliberately closed to public affairs until he had a position from which to observe human institutions from all sides.

I mentioned a fundamental bias in Emerson's thought which kept him, for a long time, from declaring for action. What was this bias? Emerson's transcendentalism is a dialectic moving between two extremes. He possessed a strong sense of the material, of property, of tradition, of history; in sum, of the accomplished fact. But he was even more a believer in spiritual values, in the reality which lies within and beyond the material. *Nature* begins with a chapter on "Commodity"—nature in its material aspects; the essay ends with "Spirit" and the prospects for the spiritualization of human life. Matter is one face of the coin; the other face is spirit. In the social sphere Emerson found this same dialectic at work. And here is the reason why, in the 1830s and 1840s, he was as much interested in the Conservative as in the Reformer. The one was necessary to the other. One preserves; the other renews. Society needs both, though both can be harmful. The Conservative brings material prosperity and benefits the arts. He may also resist ideas and impede progress. But the extreme Reformer is no better. He uses outward and vulgar means. He precipitates revolution when other measures would have done. He takes away, but what does he give? Until the fateful year 1851 Emerson saw no reason to doubt that the forces brought into play by the Conservative and the Reformer would keep America upright and in health.

Most of his observations on social affairs before 1844 are recapitulated in "Politics," which was published that year in *Essays, Second Series*. The leading ideas are familiar to anyone who has read Emerson. You can lift out its most famous sentences and reassemble the essay in a précis that states very well his achieved position at the time:

Every actual state is corrupt. Good men must not obey the laws too well. . . . The antidote to this abuse of formal government is the influence of private character, the growth of the Individual . . . The appearance of character makes the state unnecessary . . . From neither party [Conservative or Radical] has the world any benefit to expect . . . at all commensurate with the resources of the nation.

The tone of the whole essay is dispassionate. One feels, as one reads, as if Emerson had never voted or made a political speech or shaken hands with a legislator.

How different things were with him seven years later! Turn to the Concord speech on the Fugitive Slave Law and you find a new man. His state, his very house, has been invaded by an unjust law. As a citizen of Massachusetts he has been ordered to return fugitive slaves. To speak his refusal he marshals all his powers of vituperation. The speech begins quietly, but with the words of a man transformed:

Fellow Citizens: I accepted your invitation to speak to you on the great question of these days, with very little consideration of what I might have to offer: for there seems to be no option. The last year has forced us all into politics, and made it a paramount duty to seek what it is often a duty to shun. We do not breathe well. There is infamy in the air. I have a new experience. I wake in the morning with a painful sensation, which I carry about all day, and which, when traced home, is the odious remembrance of that ignominy which has fallen on Massachusetts, which robs the landscape of beauty, and takes the sunshine out of every hour.

Before he had finished, he had told his fellow Concordians that they must act. "We shall one day bring the States shoulder to shoulder and the citizens man to man to exterminate slavery." Why, in the name of the peace of mankind, do we not do this now—even if we have to impoverish the North to buy the slaves from their masters? The eyes of the nation are on Massachusetts and the South wants nothing so much as to have her entire acquiescence, as it has Boston's, to the Fugitive Slave Law.

From this moment Emerson lost his diffidence in speaking on political matters. The assault on Sumner in the Senate, the call for the relief of Kansas, the trial of John Brown, brought him to his feet in turbulent public meetings, sometimes to be howled down by southern sympathizers. As he had been, years earlier, a leader of young ministers who wished to restore beauty and joy to holiness, and to young writers who wished to create an

American "literature of the poor . . . the philosophy of the street, the meanings of household life," so now he became an inspirer of those who were ready to die, if need be, to destroy the dominance of the slave-owners in American affairs. "It is a vulgar error," he had written in his *Journal,* "to suppose that a gentleman must be ready to fight . . . Don't run amuck against the world. Have a good case to try the question on." The Emerson who could write these words in the late 1840s discovered in 1851 that the "good case to try" had been thrust upon him and he must act. The "gentleman" must be ready to fight when the precious word *liberty* had come to sound in the mouth of Webster "like the word *love* in the mouth of a courtezan."

Thoreau was never well understood by the men who knew him best. What was the man up to? Why did he waste his abundant talents? Hawthorne, who was attracted to his wildness, was puzzled by his indifference to "any systematic effort for a livelihood." Emerson was often impatient with his young friend and (as he thought) alter ego. Close as they were in the first years of their friendship, they drifted apart. Although there was never any estrangement, Emerson's persistent annoyance, which betrays a kind of uneasiness, if not guilt, breaks out many times in his journals. Henry lacked ambition, he was pugnacious and liked to say no just for the pleasure of saying no. In one of these entries Emerson, humanly but lamely, recommends the cure which men often prescribe for their friends when they think their behavior uncivilized: "He needs to fall in love, to sweeten him and straighten him."

In their mutual disgust with the low tone of American society Emerson and Thoreau were in sympathy. But even here there is a great difference. Emerson, as we have seen, was inclined to be optimistic about the future of America. Though he was amused by the reformers, he valued the radicalism which animated them. But Thoreau devotes one of his most acid passages in *Walden* to philanthropy as practiced in the America of his day:

Willard Thorp

If I knew for a certainty that a man was coming to my house with the conscious design of doing me good, I should run for my life, as from that dry and parching wind of the African deserts called the simoom . . . for fear that I should get some of his good done to me,—some of its virus mingled with my blood. . . . A man is not a good *man* to me because he will feed me if I should be starving, or warm me if I should be freezing, or pull me out of a ditch if I should ever fall into one. I can find you a Newfoundland dog that will do as much.

Thoreau could not be civil to reformers even when they were guests in the house. In June 1853 he wrote in his *Journal*:

Here have been three ultra-reformers, lecturers on Slavery, Temperance, the Church, etc., in and about our house and Mrs. Brooks's the last three or four days,—A. D. Foss, once a Baptist minister in Hopkinton, N.H.; Loring Moody, a sort of travelling pattern-working chaplain; and H. C. Wright, who shocks all the old women with his infidel writings. Though Foss was a stranger to the others, you would have thought them old and familiar cronies . . . They addressed each other constantly by their Christian names, and rubbed you continually with the greasy cheeks of their kindness. They would not keep their distance, but cuddle up and lie spoon-fashion with you, no matter how hot the weather nor how narrow the bed,—chiefly ———. I was awfully pestered with his benignity; feared I should get greased all over with it past restoration; tried to keep some starch in my clothes . . . One of the most attractive things about the flowers is their beautiful reserve.

Emerson believed that the tension between Conservative and Radical would be fruitful in the end. If some men could be wholly reformed—and it was Emerson's business to reform them—we might hope for a reformed society. In any event institutions were necessary. What he had written on this score when he was twenty, he never completely repudiated. "Institutions are a sort of homes. A man may wander long with profit, if he come home at last, but a perpetual vagrant is not honoured." These words are prophetic of what he would later think of Thoreau, the Concord saunterer, the "perpetual vagrant." Emerson was always willing to yield his small tax to the state which upholds these necessary institutions. He could say, as Thoreau would never have said: "As long as the State means you well, do not refuse your pistareen. You have a tottering cause; ninety parts of the pistareen it will spend for what you also think good, ten parts for mischief; you cannot fight heartily for a fraction." Thoreau would have denied that the state returned him even ten parts of his pistareen in good accomplished.

Everyone knows that Thoreau was a man against the state and that wherever men have appealed to the moral law as the highest law, whether they be Tolstoy in Russia or Gandhi in India, they have used Thoreau's words to help them with their argument. Emerson, too, kept the state at a distance for a time, but by the end of the 1830s he began to think and write about social questions.

Until 1854 Thoreau, in contrast to Emerson, left the state severely alone except on two occasions. As Mr. Krutch has observed, "Thoreau had never admitted, perhaps did not know, that he had 'a country,'" until, on the occasion of Anthony Burns' arrest and return to his owner, "he knew that he had lost it." But on these two earlier occasions Thoreau advocated no action; he merely (and merely is too mild a word) stated his doctrine of civil disobedience. Nor did he seek the occasions for speaking. They were thrust upon him.

In 1843 Emerson asked him to review an extraordinary and, as it turned out, prophetic little book by a German-American, J. A. Etzler's *The Paradise within the Reach of all Men, without Labour, by Powers of Nature and Machinery*. The book struck Thoreau like a whiplash. Etzler urged Americans to harness the unimagined power resources of the winds and the tides for the benefit of man. This could be done, he said, only if America cooperated in a kind of state socialism. Thoreau could imagine nothing more horrible than the enslavement of nature which Etzler so coolly advocated. Equally wicked was the proposal that men should cooperate to gain for themselves all the material blessings which Etzler promised. The sprawling industrial society of America in 1840 was bad enough. Etzler threatened to raise its potential to the nth power.

The second occasion for Thoreau's speaking out was likewise not of his own seeking. The American state which hitherto had been scarcely visible on his horizon suddenly loomed before him, abused and perverted by the comparative few who were using it to maintain slavery and kill Mexicans. It was time for all just men to sever their relations with so corrupt an instrument of man's will. Thoreau's answer was a private revolution, an anarchy with one adherent, if need be. The power of this great document, "Civil Disobedience," does not lie in its description of Thoreau's symbolic act in going to jail rather than pay a tax to an iniquitous government (Alcott had done this before him) or even in the fact that it is the classic statement of passive resistance. Its power is the power of its language. In these troubled days when committees on un-American activities are a plague in the land, Thoreau's words speak to us as sharply as they did to his first audience: "Under a government which imprisons any unjustly, the true place for a just man is also a prison."

But just as Emerson finally advanced beyond the borders of social theory so Thoreau finally advocated, not passive resistance, but action. What carried him over was the imprisonment and hanging of John Brown. If you will read his "Plea for Captain John Brown" and his "Last Days of John Brown" you will notice that the portrait of Brown has singularly Thoreauvian features. Brown was, he said, "a man of Spartan habits," who ate sparingly and fared hard as became a soldier, a "man of rare common sense and directness of speech, as of action; a transcendentalist above all, a man of ideas and principles."

A man of action—Thoreau had himself become one. You will find him writing in his *Journal* at the time: "I do not wish to kill or to be killed but I can forsee circumstances in which both these things would be unavoidable. In extremes I could even be killed." He acted against the state in December 1859, when he drove one of Brown's raiders, hidden away in Concord, to the

South Acton station so that he might escape to Canada. Not treason or revolution, but an act which could have brought him before a federal judge.

That clandestine six-mile drive from Concord to South Acton was a symbolic act of significance in Thoreau's private life, but we know that five years earlier, in 1854, he had published a book which would prove to be a subversive act with continuous consequences. *Walden* is not merely an indictment of the gold-hunting, property-burdened America of Thoreau's day. What it teaches can change men's lives, bringing them abruptly before the basic "economic" questions: Is my life of the devil or of God? How can I put my house in order (arrange my "economy") so that I can discover whether my life—the life of the soul—is mean or if it is sublime? How can I live deep so that I can suck out all the marrow of life and put to rout all that is not life? Life is what we are given and we must be able, in the end, to give our account of it. Most men conduct their affairs so that in their pursuit of "necessaries" they choke off the life of the soul. In the end they will have nothing to report. They will not have explored even the first economic problem—the theory of value.

As Emerson and Thoreau moved from social thought to social action, so Whitman moved from action to thought during the years in which he meditated and matured the first *Leaves of Grass*. He had been a party man, a member of the left wing of the Democrats. Between 1842 and 1859 he lectured the citizens of Brooklyn in scores of editorials on their duties as members of a great city and a great democracy. It surprises one, therefore, to turn from these hard-biting, practical editorials to the dozen sprawling poems which make up the 1855 *Leaves of Grass*. Can this be the same man speaking? No thunder here about Douglas and Buchanan, outrages on emigrant ships, criminal abortions, or British rule in India.

What had happened was simple enough. Whitman the crusading editor had become Whitman the bard, attempting in a new literary medium to awaken his readers to a more fundamental need than the reforms he had called for in the various papers he edited. If American democracy was to endure, then Americans must be given a faith which would make it endure. In his own way he was now demanding what Emerson and Thoreau had for a long time called for—a purification of the democratic faith.

Be at peace bloody flukes of doubters and sullen mopers,
I take my place among you as much as among any;
The past is the push of you and me all precisely the same,
And the day and night are for you and me and all,
And what is yet untried and afterward is for you and me and all.

I do not know what is untried and afterward,
But I know it is sure and alive and sufficient.

Each who passes is considered, and each who stops is considered,
    and not a single one can it fail.

It cannot fail the young man who died and was buried,
Nor the young woman who died and was put by his side. . . .
Nor the present, nor the least wisp that is known.

It was this surging faith that American democracy could purify itself which so affected Emerson and impelled him to write his famous letter to Whitman. The poem meets, he said, "the demand I am always making of what seems the sterile and stingy Nature, as if too much handiwork, or too much lymph in the temperament were making our Western wits fat and mean."

Even Thoreau's reserve gave way before the "something a little more than human" that he found in Whitman. Repelled at first by Walt's egoism and sensuality, on meeting him he yielded to the power that overwhelmed Emerson. *Leaves of Grass,* Thoreau wrote, "sounds to me very brave and American . . . an alarum or trumpet-note ringing through the American camp."

Sixteen years later, sobered by his failure to reach the ear of the people and by the national tragedy of civil war, Whitman attempted to look far into the future of America in a now neglected book, *Democratic Vistas.* It is surely one of the fundamental American works, as basic for students of politics as *Walden* should be for economists. Whitman saw as clearly what was rotten in post Civil War America as Thoreau had seen what was wrong with American society in the 1840s. Many of the problems he states would be problems, to be solved by experiment, to New Dealers sixty years later. But the concluding thesis of the book is Whitman's continued call for

powerful native philosophs and orators and bards . . . as rallying points to come, in times of danger, and to fend off ruin and defection . . . Unwieldy and immense, who shall hold in behemoth? who bridle leviathan? Flaunt it as we choose, athwart and over the roads of our progress loom huge uncertainty and dreadful, threatening gloom . . . Democracy grows rankly up the thickest, noxious, deadliest plants and fruits of all—brings worse and worse invaders—needs newer, larger, stronger, keener compensations and compellers.

His call for the "compellers" has been answered, else how should you and I be safely here? Where does the democratic faith live and speak to men if not in the pages of *My Antonia* and *For Whom the Bell Tolls* and *The Grapes of Wrath?*

Though Melville wrote only one piece which deals directly with social questions—the brief supplement to his war poems, *Battle-Pieces* (1866)—his thinking about the relations of the individual to society was continuous from the mid-forties until his death in 1891. Every one of his important works, from *Typee* to *Billy Budd,* contains, by inference or symbol, a social theme. Except for Whitman, he was the most ardent democrat of the writers of the mid-century. He was wary of patrician democrats like Cooper who believed that leadership should be in the hands of the natural aristocracy, by virtue of their education and desire to serve the state. He even suspected his friend Hawthorne of belonging to this group and told him so politely in 1851.

The heroes of Melville's early works are not patrician democrats but men of the people like Jack Chase or Captain Ahab. Yet almost from the beginning Melville entertained doubts about equalitarianism which Whitman experienced twenty years later in *Democratic Vistas.* His ardent faith in the common man speaks through the two "Knights and Squires" chapters of *Moby Dick*. But in *Mardi* he had warned these "sovereign kings" of democracy about the dangers of an unthinking trust in the American state:

Freedom is more social than political. And its real felicity is not to be shared. *That* is of a man's own individual getting and holding. It is not, who rules the state, but who rules me. Better be secure under one king, than exposed to violence from twenty millions of monarchs, though oneself be of the number.

This seeming contradiction can be reconciled if we explore Melville's mind a little. In his early years he was an extreme humanist, believing passionately in the innate dignity of man. That was why his whole being cried out when he saw men flogged on board an American warship. The lash which touched the body violated the image of God.

But for all his reverence before the godliness in man, he recognized the depravity in human beings and the consequent fallibility of an extreme democracy. In *Mardi* Melville pictured his ideal state, Serenia, but it is no utopia like that in William Morris' *News from Nowhere*:

It is imperfect; and long must so remain. But we make not the miserable many support the happy few . . . By the abounding, the needy are supplied. Yet not from statute, but from the dictates, born half dormant in us, and warmed into life by Alma [Christ]. These dictates we but follow in all we do; we are not dragged to righteousness; but go running . . . The vicious we make dwell apart, until reclaimed . . . The sin of others rests not upon our heads: none we drive to crime.

Eight years after publishing these measured words about man's capability for self-government, Melville had swung to the low point in his thinking about society. There are no knights or squires, no Jack Chases or Ahabs in *The Confidence Man*. Society is made up of the cheaters and the cheated, the confidence men and their victims. The mutual trust between men which holds a society together has turned to greed and suspicion. Twenty years later Melville had worked himself out of this bitterness. In his long poem *Clarel* (1876) he is ready to examine once more, and minutely, as he had done in *Mardi* with a youthful exuberance, the social and ethical problems of this later time. The very openness of the long discussions in the poems shows that Melville was on the way to a solution of the problem which had always vexed him: how can fallible man control the depravity to which civilization is peculiarly prone? Although he permits one of his characters, Ungar, who fought for the South in the Civil War, to say more savage things about American democracy than Thoreau ever uttered, the poem ends on a note of hope.

> Degrees we know, unknown in days before;
> The light is greater, hence the shadow more.

Finally, in *Billy Budd,* Melville struck a balance and found the point at which he could come to rest. As I read the story, he is saying to us that the society we live in is and always will be a world at war. There must be discipline and order to hold off the enemy from without and hold down the enemy within. Occasionally all that is fine and innocent, like Billy Budd who is impressed from a ship significantly called the *Rights of Man,* will suffer injustice under the discipline which keeps the ship in fighting trim. But man never forgets the myth of his lost innocence or his intuitions of the higher justice of which it is a part. There can be no order without sacrifice, but the sacrifice haunts the imaginations of men so that they perpetually remember how costly in human life is the stability of society.

We should take note of one other theme in *Billy Budd* because it brings Melville close to Emerson and Thoreau when they decided at length to come to terms with society and to act, if need be, to preserve the state. Captain Vere might have avoided his responsibility in condemning Billy to death. But he neither agrees with his officers, who would do nothing, nor passes the responsibility to a higher authority. He tells the court what their duty is. "Our vowed responsibility is in this: That however pitilessly [the] law may operate, we nevertheless adhere to it and administer it." There is more than an echo here of Emerson's "The last year has . . . made it a paramount duty to seek what it is often a duty to shun" and of Thoreau's "I do not wish to kill or be killed but I can forsee circumstances in which both these things would be unavoidable."

What brings Emerson, Thoreau, Whitman, and Melville together is that as writers in a democratic society they tried to live their lives with principle. They did not shirk what Melville's Captain Vere calls man's "vowed responsibility." They were realists in their social thinking. They were all aware of what Melville names the "depravity according to nature" which works through evil men to destroy what good men try to do. But not even Whitman and Melville, who observed the degradation of American democracy in the last quarter of the last century, lost their faith in the possibility of its recovery.

Finally, it will be instructive, I think, to put beside these four men the altogether dissimilar case of Mark Twain. For he was a democratic man who never found, and indeed never sought, the principle which animated the faith of the other four. In the beginning Mark Twain took for granted the accomplishments of American democracy. Europe was a fraud; only in America was social progress assured. He was moved, of course, to satirize the political corruption and the speculative mania of the Gilded Age. What animates *Huckleberry Finn* is Mark Twain's own decency and his hatred of hypocrisy and slavery and petty tyranny. He could always be counted on to help a social cause and he always lined up on the right side. But, as we now know, in the end Mark Twain lost his faith in humanity and his bitterness was even blacker than Melville's when he wrote *The Confidence Man.* The entries in his notebooks during the last years come back constantly to the theme of the damned human race.

"The skin of every human being contains a slave."

"The only very marked difference between the average civilized man and the average savage is that the one is gilded and the other painted."

"In any civic crisis of a great and dangerous sort the common herd is not privately anxious about the rights and wrongs of the matter, it is only anxious to be on the winning side."

Among these many black commentaries one entry strikes me as most interesting in the light of what the other men stood for: "We have thrown away the most valuable asset we have—the individual right to oppose both flag and country when he (just *he* by himself) believes them to be in the wrong. We have thrown it away; and with it all that was really respectable about that grotesque and laughable word, Patriotism."

Who had thrown away this most valuable asset? Not Mark Twain's friend Howells. Not Frank Norris or Dreiser (for we are now in the twentieth century). It was Twain himself who had thrown it away by refusing to speak and to act. He imprisoned his despair over "man's essential cowardice, pettiness and evil" inside himself and in the end this despair produced a block which prevented him from completing the scores of manuscripts which piled up around him.

This spectacle of Mark Twain's debacle, the collapse into despair of a man who had come to be the symbol the world over of the successful democratic man, is only the first of such dispiriting "cases." We now know this type well: the liberal who is not the tough realist that Emerson was or Thoreau was and who in the end turns his guns on the democratic society from which he had hoped too much. If he had, in his idealistic period, a popular following you will find him now in Mr. Luce's stable of well-fed hacks. If he was a more esoteric writer in his happier days, you will find him vending his misanthropy in the *Partisan Review*. These sour liberals might profit by a little instruction from our social realists. They might be brought to agree with the surprising but comforting conclusion to Thoreau's great indictment of American democracy, "Life without Principle":

Politics is, as it were, the gizzard of society, full of grit and gravel, and the two political parties are its two opposite halves,— sometimes split into quarters, it may be, which grind on each other. Not only individuals, but states, have thus a confirmed

104

dyspepsia, which expresses itself, you can imagine by what sort of eloquence. Thus our life is not altogether a forgetting, but also, alas! to a great extent, a remembering, of that which we should never have been conscious of, certainly not in our waking hours. Why should we not meet, not always as dyspeptics, to tell our bad dreams, but sometimes as *eu*peptics, to congratulate each other on the ever-glorious morning? I do not make an exorbitant demand, surely.

◄ CLARENCE GOHDES ►

The Reception of Some Nineteenth-Century American Authors in Europe

ONE of the important reasons for the vast interchange of books among nations during the nineteenth century was the growth in the supply of readers at such an accelerated pace that local production was taxed to meet its demands. Reprints of older works and of new books by foreign authors had a vogue much larger than ever before simply because of the needs of the enormously increased horde of readers. Their number, it should be remembered, developed even more rapidly than did the population at large. The publishers of books, magazines, and newspapers in Western Europe found themselves faced with an insufficient supply of literary materials to satisfy particularly the multitudes of children and mentally juvenile adults who suddenly clamored for the wherewithal to gratify the craving for instruction and entertainment in print which the popularization of schooling had helped to bring on. The comparatively aristocratic methods of publication, inherited from the days of relatively few readers, gave way before what might be called a democratization of the book world. In England, for example, publishers guessed that the last quarter of the century was marked by a trebling or even a quadrupling of book readers. Something similar is very conspicuous at present in Russia, where a determined and all-powerful government has taken over the whole business of publishing and has attempted to make it fit not only the demands of propaganda but also the demands of untold multitudes of newly created readers. One of the results has been that between

1918 and 1943 translations were made in Russia of 217 American authors, with total sales of about thirty-seven million copies.

From the outset, American literary production was largely by the people, for the people. The newspaper and the magazine flourished here as nowhere else in the world, and they continue to do so. Moreover, all our authors were from the ranks considered in Europe as middle or lower class, and they wrote for persons much like themselves. Thus the American author was a producer of the very kind of literature that was most needed in Europe, and as a result his offerings were likely to cross the Atlantic as soon as they made themselves evident. The central picture, then, of our impact as a literary nation upon the world at large is that of our popular authors finding abroad an audience similar to the one for which they wrote at home. People are much alike all over the globe in reacting to the appeal of the sentimental, the humorous, the thrilling, the shocking, or the morally elevating; and in all these emotional-intellectual areas our country has produced an ample supply. It was true in the day of Irving and Cooper; it is true in the time of Sinclair Lewis, of the author of the Tarzan stories, and of the perpetrators of the so-called comic books.

While the arbiters of taste and culture in Europe, usually conditioned by the antidemocratic bias of the upper classes, early proclaimed the impossibility of artistic or even intellectual accomplishment above the level of applied science in the New World, their hostility was gradually undermined by the democratization of the book trade within the bounds of their own countries; yet it was conventional throughout the century to dismiss American productions as rarely worthy of serious critical evaluation. This attitude vitally affected the course of highbrow criticism in the United States itself, and Americans of astute nature and advanced education sometimes have waited until a European sanction was forthcoming before respecting the accomplishments of their own brethren. Something of this attitude still lingers, though it is rapidly tobogganing down a very steep hill.

The American Writer and the European Tradition

Though critics abroad—and many of their American compeers—in general presented a force unfavorable to the reception of American books by other nations, their effect was small, for in most cases formal criticism has nothing to do with the popularity of a work until years after that work has exerted its first appeal. Furthermore, a very special circumstance existed during most of the century which was so favorable for American products that critical opposition had no more power than an empty barrel in a cataract. I refer to the absence of an international copyright act. While Congress as early as 1790 had passed regulations protecting within the United States most works called "literary" which were written by nationals, until 1891 it made no provision whatever to protect the foreign author. As a result, not only did European books swarm in cheap editions on the American market but American works swarmed on the bookmarts of Europe. Piracy, or unauthorized publication, was the rule until 1891, and of course the European publisher leaped at the opportunity to supply his clamoring new readers with material that cost him not one cent for authors' fees. Often a foreign newspaper or magazine editor simply reprinted something from America whenever he found anything suited to his needs. Sometimes the work was garbled, its title changed, its authorship unidentified. The same was true even with books. As a consequence, no one will ever be able to make a complete listing of all the American poems, essays, and stories which found their way into periodicals or books abroad.

In the effort to obtain remuneration from British publishers, many American books were published in England before their first appearance in New York, Boston, or Philadelphia, or appeared simultaneously on the two continents. In general, the writers of these works were likely to be such favorites with the British that London firms were willing to make payments for early publication so as to reap the harvest before the competition of pirates could diminish profits. And from time to time prior publication within the British domain was considered sufficient qualification to warrant copyright by aliens. Among such works first brought out in London are Emerson's *Representative Men* (1850), Melville's *Moby Dick* (1851), which was called *The Whale* in its first English edition, and Mark Twain's *Tom Sawyer* (1876), *Life on the Mississippi* (1883), and *Huckleberry Finn* (1884). Thirty titles by James Fenimore Cooper are thought to have had English priority, six by Washington Irving, and thirteen or fourteen by Longfellow. Of course those Americans who lived for a long while in England, Bret Harte and Henry James, for example, issued a goodly number of their works under the initial auspices of London firms. One advantage of such legitimate publication in England was that these books were likely to enjoy better critical attention in reputable journals than that which they might have received if they had been merely reprints. As a rule, reprints, whether authorized or pirated, rarely attracted much critical notice, and this fact easily explains why the history of the consumption of American books in Europe is not revealed by the history of their critical fate.

Because there was no need for translation, because the general nature of American literature was so similar to that of British literature, and because business traffic of all sorts was so close between Boston and New York on the one hand and Liverpool and London on the other, more American works were printed or reprinted in Great Britain than in any other European country. It is quite possible that a number of our literary products were for a time more widely read there than at home. Just as Dickens had more readers in the United States than in his own land, so Hawthorne and Longfellow during the 1850s were probably more popular in England. Henry Adams' novel *Democracy* (1880) most assuredly was more popular in England, and in Germany a translation went into a fifth edition by 1885. During most of the century the British consumed more contemporary literature from the United States than from all the rest of the world combined.

England is the most important country for the study of American literature abroad not only because of this fact but also because the chief knowledge of current American books came to

Germany and France and in part even to Russia via the London market. British publishers were closer to the source of supply, had for years been the sole providers of literary works in the English language, and had well-established connections for the exchange of copyrights with important Continental firms. Outside of England the most valued series of books in the English language was the Tauchnitz library, published in Leipzig. When it began to include Americans among its authors—which it did very early—it regularly looked to London firms to arrange for the supply, and it continued to call its series Collection of British Authors. Up to June 1914, 68 of its 490 authors were Americans. Publishers in France and probably in Italy, too, were supplied with information about likely prospects for translation through agents in the British capital.

No one can say positively whether Germany or France was next in importance for the distribution of American literature in Europe. My own guess would be Germany. From Germany knowledge of our books went quickly to Austria and Switzerland—and less directly to the Scandinavian countries. France was of course the natural intermediary through which knowledge of our offerings was transmitted to the Italians, the Spanish, the Portuguese, and, last but not least, the Latin Americans. At the present time New York is the chief center for the foreign trade in American books.

As yet, we have not had sufficient investigation—especially of the bibliographical sort—of the impact of American books on the Continent to permit more than tentative general conclusions. But in all likelihood, except for Benjamin Franklin, who was known earlier, our literary men came to the knowledge of the European reader through the initial trickle of their works published in the 1820s. During the fifties there was more general recognition. After the Civil War, which was of course widely publicized abroad, the conventional critical prejudice against American intellectual pretensions was somewhat mitigated because of the failure of the dire prophecies of the European upper classes, and the consumption of American books steadily rose with the increase in the number of readers. The international copyright act in 1891 temporarily diminished the number of new American works brought out in Europe but did not check the reprinting of older favorites.

During the present century the continued vogue of American works has been enhanced most notably by the two world wars, which have not only established the United States as a world power of first magnitude but have so interfered with British literary production that our nation has taken over as probably the chief source of new foreign works in English. That *Gone with the Wind* has been the most widely heralded novel of its sort throughout the contemporary world is no more remarkable than that the Nobel Prize has honored several of our authors or that in Italy at the present time a Sicilian named Elio Vittorini betrays the manifest influence of Ernest Hemingway.

Early in the nineteenth century the novels of our first valued fictionist, Charles Brockden Brown, were reprinted in England and were known to Keats, Scott, Hazlitt, and Shelley, the last-mentioned being very enthusiastic about one of Brown's heroines. Of any vogue on the Continent I know nothing. After Brown there soon appeared the works of Irving, William Ellery Channing, Bryant, and Cooper, who may be said to have established the existence of an American literature both at home and in Europe. All these men were reprinted in England, and except for Bryant, who has never figured importantly outside the United States, they basked there in a favor equal to their reception at home. Bryant's poems were of course pilfered by the British periodicals, and some of his work in book form appeared in England and Germany, but he exerted no great appeal.

The acceptance of Irving was far different, for with the publication of *The Sketch Book* he was immediately welcomed as an esteemed aspirant to literary honors, British publishers paid him as well as they did Byron, and his essays outranked those of Charles Lamb in popularity. As a result of all the enthusiasm in England, *The Sketch Book* and *Bracebridge Hall,* his next work, were quickly translated into French and German. A set of his collected works began to appear in Frankfurt in 1826, and in France there were at least thirty-eight separate editions of one or the other of his books by 1842.

In Spain Irving never proved to be famous, in spite of his use of Spanish material. Selections from his charming *The Alhambra* were published as early as 1833, the year following its first appearance, but there was, apparently, no complete version before 1888. An American-Iberian named George Washington Montgomery adapted certain tales from *The Sketch Book* about 1829, but the results strike us now as mere curiosities. In one of the adaptations Rip Van Winkle becomes a native of Granada who goes hunting in the Sierras with a company of Moorish horsemen and falls asleep after partaking of some oriental sweetmeats. Astonishing as that may seem, it still falls short of equaling another Spanish version which pictures Rip as finally returning to his village only to discover his wife in the arms of another man. This "French" touch may help us to remember that, for the most part, Spanish knowledge of Irving came via Paris. Of all Irving's books probably his biography of Columbus (1821) had the widest circulation on the Continent. The Spaniards alone brought out four editions up to 1854, and no one knows exactly how many there were elsewhere.

Fenimore Cooper was much more generally read. In Spain he was possibly the chief American author of his century, and in 1853 a Spanish critic scarcely exceeded the limitations of truth when he declared that *El último de los Mohicanos* "is a masterpiece which has become a classic in every language of Europe." Twenty years earlier, Samuel Morse had written:

I have visited, in Europe, many countries, and what I have asserted of the fame of Mr. Cooper I assert from personal knowledge. In every city of Europe that I visited the works of Cooper were conspicuously placed in the windows of every bookshop. They are published as soon as he produces them in thirty-four different places in Europe. They have been seen by American travelers in the languages of Turkey and Persia, in Constantinople, in Egypt, at Jerusalem, at Ispahan.

The Spy and *The Pioneers* appeared in German editions in 1824, and by the middle of the century there were probably a hundred other editions of Cooper in book form in that language.

Like Balzac and Dumas *père* in France, Goethe also was an avid reader. Before 1807 he had no real knowledge of the New World, but during the 1820s he followed eagerly the numerous articles on America printed in a Parisian journal named *Le Globe.* Like many another unwise wise man, he questioned whether such an immigrant nation as ours would ever acquire a fundamentally original character. After reading reviews of Irving and Cooper, he penned a poem to the United States in which he expressed his belief that America "had it better" than Europe and advised any poets that might come in our future to avoid the old romantic themes of the Continent. His interest in our authors seems to have been confined to Franklin, Irving, and Cooper, and it was the New World background that he sought to find in their works. Of Cooper he read not only the novels but the social criticisms as well, and he even dipped into Ramsay's *History of the American Revolution* to acquaint himself with the historical background treated in *The Spy.* In 1826, after appreciating *The Pioneers,* he expressed an admiration for Cooper's technique, which he compared with that of other great novelists. He may have borrowed a few suggestions for the composition of his own *Novelle.* Anyone curious about the matter will find the inevitable German dissertation on the subject: Spiridion Wukadinovic, *Goethes Novelle, der Schauplatz, Coopersche Einflusz* (Halle, 1909).

As in the United States, Cooper's influence is to be seen in a variety of authors who followed his trail into a wilderness peopled by Indians and scouts. It may even be, as a Spanish encyclopedia averred, that he "did a great deal to encourage emigration, in Germany, as well as in England." Certainly he gave a new thrill to the readers of romance, and he caused many a family to warn an emigrating relative to beware of losing his scalp when he ventured west from New York City. The exciting new background of the frontier accounted for much—but not all—of Cooper's appeal throughout Europe. And, we may add here, when Bret Harte came along with his stories of a glamorous West, he found much the same favor. *Gabriel Conroy,* Harte's only long novel, had six different editions in Austria or Germany within a year, in addition to the Tauchnitz text in English. Of course the call of the wild was later heard in the offerings of Jack London, Zane Grey, and James Oliver Curwood, not to mention the movies and the vast collection of dime novels which the Germans call "revolver literature."

An even greater sensation than Cooper's novels, for it was more concentrated, came with Mrs. Stowe's *Uncle Tom's Cabin,* which within two years attracted in England the most astonishing sales witnessed up to that time. Nothing by Scott or Dickens had ever tapped such an immediate torrent of popularity. Within a few months after a pirate issued it in London, in April 1852, more than a million and a half copies were sold by the forty publishers who printed it in Great Britain. The London *Times,* atrabilious about all things American, forgot most of its accustomed sneers for the nonce and gave it three and a half columns, stating that one out of every three travelers on the trains was to be seen with the book in his hands. As late as 1891 an investigator of books read by British peasants found the four works most frequently present in the cottages of "well-to-do laborers" to be *Pilgrim's Progress,* Foxe's *Book of Martyrs, Uncle Tom's Cabin,* and *The Wide, Wide World,* this last also by an American, Susan Warner. Such a phenomenon as *Uncle Tom's* success in London was naturally not overlooked by Continental publishers, and soon the antislavery classic was serialized in newspapers in Stockholm and Paris, and translations in book form cropped up all over the world. It is said that the tale has appeared in more than twenty languages, including a Hindu dialect and Javanese.

Of the several later nineteenth-century American novels that followed Mrs. Stowe's into almost worldwide popularity probably the most spectacular were *Looking Backward* (1888) by

Edward Bellamy and *In His Steps* (1896) by the Reverend Charles Monroe Sheldon. The latter is a humble tale of how a modern clergyman followed the example of Jesus in his daily tasks. It has been translated into at least twenty-three languages or dialects, and its total sale is reckoned anywhere from five to twenty millions. One should perhaps mention also Lew Wallace's *Ben-Hur*, which ran through 132 "editions" within twenty-three years for one Stuttgart publisher alone.

In England at the same time that Uncle Tom's nobility was on everyone's lips, Longfellow was the poet whose volumes were in most demand. Until recently British people, wherever they live, have purchased more copies of his books than they have of Tennyson or Browning. Hosts of poetasters, more rarely real poets, were incited to activity by him. His influence upon the English was of great importance, nevertheless, for he came to many a young person at a critical time and inspired an enduring taste for the pleasures to be found in verse. Longfellow's bust stands in Westminster Abbey, near Dryden's and Chaucer's, for various reasons. One of the chief, no doubt, was the recollection by many a middle-aged Englishman of what "A Psalm of Life" or *Evangeline* had meant to him in his youth. Here is an illustrative statement:

I bought cheap editions of Milton and Burns and religiously read them through at the age of twelve, though as yet with no great relish. Longfellow, whom I also bought in a corresponding sixpenny edition, was the first poet to make a profound and intimate impression upon me. Here for the first time, especially in the more lyrical poems, I seemed to hear a living voice which spoke to me in the language of my own heart. Longfellow was, as it were, the sweet friend of my early boyhood, the only friend I then possessed with whom I could privately commune. My love for him was later submerged in a mightier love for Shelley— though in the first tempestuous spring of adolescence I revelled in the intoxicating poetry of Alexander Smith's *Life-Dreams* and Mrs. Browning's *Aurora Leigh*—but there always remained with me, long after I outgrew his poems, a tender memory for that first friend of wistful and pensive puberty. No other writer so well expressed in my day the ideas and emotions of that period.

This is a passage from the autobiography of Havelock Ellis, a man whose name, surely, is not often thought of in connection with Longfellow "fans."

Just as Longfellow was the most widely known of our poets in Great Britain, so he was also in the rest of the world. The fifteen or more translations of *Evangeline* in German, the half dozen or more renderings in Spanish, including one by a Mexican and another by a Chilean, merely illustrate the extent of his vogue. It can never really be measured. The almost unbelievable popularity of certain of his shorter lyrics, like "A Psalm of Life," from which Baudelaire filched a few lines, or "Excelsior," which carried the motto of New York State around the globe, is mirrored in the translations which Argentina school texts include. "Excelsior" has been memorized by many a student in the secondary schools of Italy, where shopkeepers and even bootblacks have named their establishments in its honor. Longfellow was known from Iceland to Australia, and the Russian Ivan Bunin (Nobel laureate in 1933) is probably as well recognized for his translation of *Hiawatha* as for any of his original works. Altogether, it is quite possible that Longfellow was, and maybe still is, the best known minor poet who ever wrote in the English language. Oxford and Cambridge gladly gave him an honorary degree.

In Great Britain especially, but also in Germany and elsewhere, our humorists long ago were hailed as contributing an ample and original store of mirth. The list of our writers who qualified as fun-makers seemed unlimited. Irving, Holmes, Lowell, and a whole procession of minor newspaper drolls carried chuckles across the Atlantic before the 1860s, but after the Civil War a veritable deluge of humor poured forth. European publishers brought out not only single volumes but whole series of books by "American humorists." Mark Twain, of course, was the foremost.

His visits to various European countries occasioned newspaper publicity astonishing in quantity and fervor, and the celebration in 1935 of his centenary was by no means confined to his native land. Sales of his books in German-speaking areas from 1874 to 1937 are estimated at more than a million copies, and in Russia from 1918 to 1943 more than three million of his books were sold. Only Jack London, with ten million copies in 567 editions, has surpassed the author of *Huckleberry Finn* in Soviet Russia. School editions of *The Prince and the Pauper* have appeared since the nineties in Germany, a sure sign of approval. Mark Twain, however, presents difficulties to the foreigner. A Russian once told me how he and his brother tried in vain to imagine what it was like to play Tom Sawyer's game called "hookey." Not until they came to live in New York did they find out. If Whitman's line "I *loafe* and invite my soul" is made to read "I *eat* and invite my soul" by the standard translation of *Leaves of Grass* in Italy, what must some of the renderings of Mark Twain's lusty Americanisms be like!

Thus far, we have concerned ourselves primarily with illustrating by means of nineteenth-century authors how our literature of the people made its way to a fitting audience in Europe. (I do not mean to suggest, however, that the writers we have thus far considered were altogether without influence above the plane of the masses or of such European authors as sought a similar hearing.) But perhaps we may profitably complete our study with an illustration or two of the vogue of American authors in more intellectual quarters. Whitman, reluctantly, I exclude.

We may use Emerson as our first example. While there can be little question that the humbler attendants upon Mechanics' Institutes supplied an important element among the audiences in twenty-five cities who listened to one or more of the sixty-odd lectures which he delivered in England in 1847–48, it is also true that collegians and professors were stirred by his catalytic agency. In the middle of the century the halls of Oxford resounded with his name, and in 1874 the students at the University of Glasgow nominated him for the office of lord-rector of their institution, an honor previously held by Edmund Burke, Adam Smith, and

Macaulay. Four years later, one of the London publishing houses, inspired by *Representative Men,* planned a work on *The Hundred Greatest Men* and, in asking Emerson to write the general introduction, said that there were only two persons fit for the task, "the two Fathers of the Century Mr. Emerson and Mr. Carlyle." They preferred the former as being more catholic.

Later, when John Lubbock selected his famous "one hundred best books," few British intellectuals found fault with the inclusion of the Sage of Concord, Massachusetts. The circle of friends who fortified the youthful mind of George Eliot were Emersonians almost without exception, and she herself called him the "first *man* I have ever seen." Clough, Froude, Sterling, Spencer, Tyndall, Huxley—all were among the distinguished ranks of those who owed him a debt for stimulus and spiritual refreshment. Matthew Arnold's devotion is expressed not only in an early sonnet but also in a lecture on Emerson. Therein he recalled the season of his youth at Oxford, when Newman, Carlyle, and Goethe joined with a clear voice from New England to inspire and encourage. Arnold coupled Emerson's name with that of Marcus Aurelius as "the friend and aider of those who would live in the spirit," adding: "As Wordsworth's poetry is, in my judgment, the most important work done in verse, in our language, during the present century, so Emerson's *Essays* are, I think, the most important work done in prose."

Elsewhere in Europe the evidence of Emerson's impact upon minds of higher stature is not as abundant as it is in Great Britain; in translation Emerson inevitably loses his most striking quality—his aphoristic brilliance. Nevertheless, here and there the signs are not lacking. Among the authors who employed the French language one finds such attentive readers as the Swiss Amiel, whose esteemed journal was his chief gift to letters. There can be no doubt about his careful pondering of Emerson during the middle of the century, for his journal mentions his encounter with the ideas of "the Stoic of a young America" (in the entry for February 1, 1852). Edgar Quinet was also a careful reader. Adam Mickiewicz, greatest of Polish Romantic poets, lent him a copy of Emerson's *Nature* as early as 1838, two years after it first appeared. Professors at the Collège de France inspiring the 1848 principles included a few Emersonians, and in 1878 Emerson became a member of the Institut de France. Such vogue as Emerson had in France must have been largely in the ranks of advanced liberals among the Protestants. Similarities with certain of the views of Henri Bergson are palpable enough, but it is not at all clear that the philosopher was really indebted to Emerson. One does not need to speculate about the tumultuous privacy of the creative mind to ascertain Emerson's effect upon Maurice Maeterlinck, for the Belgian has acknowledged it. "Behold Emerson," says the author of *Pelléas et Mélisande,* "the good morning shepherd of pale meadows, green with a new optimism, both natural and plausible . . . He came for many just when he should have come, and just when they had need of new explanations."

In Germany Emerson also came at a good moment to Nietzsche. Heading the list of authors *gelesen am meisten* in Nietzsche's journal for 1863 stands the name of the essayist whose works he ransacked for his notebook and whose thoughts are occasionally woven into his letters as well as into *Also sprach Zarathustra* (1883–92). Even Unamuno has at least once been called, by a Spanish critic, an "imitator" of Emerson. In the last analysis, however, Emersonianism breeds the giant that destroys itself, in its very insistence upon self-reliance. Moreover, its course is hard to trace in the currents of eclectic idealism. Who can ever track down the origins of a neoplatonic generality or a mystical intuition? In these areas of thinking the mind, indeed, as well as the soul, "knows no persons."

Whatever the actual nature of Emerson's influence upon the minds of Europe, in all probability the effect of Poe was greater. I do not mean in such comparatively small matters as the echoes of his poems in the verses of Tennyson, Baudelaire, Rimbaud, Samain, or Paul Valéry. Nor do I mean in the obvious influence of his very popular tales on such diverse writers as Robert Louis Stevenson, Villiers de L'Isle-Adam, Joris Huysmans (in *A*

Rebours), or Jules Verne. Indeed, one can scarcely think of a master in the field of the pseudoscientific tale or the story of the macabre since the middle of the nineteenth century who has *not* owed a debt to Poe. What I refer to especially is the profound results of Poe's esthetic principles upon the progress of the theories of literature. Look where you will among the creeds of Parnassians, Symbolists, Surrealists, or their offshoots anywhere in Europe and you are likely to discover results of the reading of Poe. That this fact is due largely to the genius of the French—more especially, to the almost fantastic adoration of Charles Baudelaire—in no way minimizes the contribution of Poe. While the world at large knows Longfellow best of all our poets, and now probably ranks Whitman as our most eminent genius in verse, there can be little doubt that Poe has transcended both in his importance to literature as an art. Compared with him Henry James thus far has been mere "feathers."

It is one of the ironies of history that the nation so long despised by the highbrows of Europe as paltry in intellect, feeble in art, and dangerous in politics should have contributed through Poe to the world's store of sophisticated critical theory. In a way, it is almost as big a joke as Sydney Smith's notorious question, "Who reads an American book?"

American Naturalism: Reflections
from Another Era

WITH us naturalism has been not so much a school as a climate
of feeling, almost in the very air of our modern American life,
with its mass patterns, its rapid social changes, its idolatry of the
mechanical and of "facts." The French may have conceived *le
roman naturalist,* but Chicago, many an American writer has
suspected, is its incarnation. And while the term is inevitable to
our discussion of the twentieth-century American novel—it
evokes for us a particular concentration on "society," from Frank
Norris and Theodore Dreiser to John Dos Passos and James T.
Farrell; it establishes a dividing line between temperaments in
the novel (certainly it is hard to think of Hemingway and
Faulkner as "naturalists," their sensibility is too wide)—it will
not help us much to trace its intellectual pedigree too solemnly,
to follow its track, in the usual academic way, out of literature
into the history of "influences."

The influences are there; they are still here, in the life all
around us. Naturalism in America is not easily reduced to the
well-known formula of determinism with its pretensions to "laws"
of human behavior, its severe air of necessary meanness. Think
only of the career of Theodore Dreiser, the most deeply grounded
of our naturalistic novelists, with whose *Sister Carrie* (1900)
so much of our twentieth-century social fiction seems to begin.

Stephen Crane, exactly his contemporary, and Frank Norris,
only a year older, were writing "naturalism" before him, but for
them it was still in the experimental mode. Crane's *Maggie*

(1893), almost too pointedly subtitled *A Girl of the Streets,* comes out of the world of Jacob Riis' *How the Other Half Lives*; it is a social exposé and rather a trick, the book of a precocious and restless young reporter who has found an untouched subject in the slums. It has nothing of the daemonic sincerity of *The Red Badge of Courage.* Frank Norris' *McTeague* (1899) is powerful, and as we so often say of the characters in the naturalistic novel, "tragic," for we still have no other word for it; but there is something curiously repellent about this novel, not because of its subject, but because it is so obviously patronizing toward the "common" and "brutal" materials he has chosen. Morally Norris is not *in* his book at all, just as Crane, led to *Maggie* by its scandalousness, is not in his; everything seems just a little too deliberately planned; he has been reading Zola, and without anything of Zola's humanity, would like to manipulate tragic destinies; he is ironic, superior, and rather coldly intent on squeezing all the horror out of the situation and his characters—whom, in fact, he has chosen because they are so "primitive," either in their grossness (McTeague) or their piteousness (Trina), rather than for anything felt in their characters. As soon as we turn to *Sister Carrie,* however, we know that we are in the presence of a writer for whom naturalism is the only way of addressing himself to life. He found an impalpable emotion arising from the very commonplaceness of human existence.

Dreiser had been a newspaperman writing Sunday-supplement human interest stories; he was now a novelist, but only as he had found in himself the courage to believe that his kind of life could be brought into the novel. It was a belief that came slowly and painfully, and one he was to lose for a time after *Sister Carrie* so shocked his publisher's wife that she had the entire first edition withdrawn from circulation. In many ways he was closer to the worldly, driven, inarticulate characters in his novel than to sophisticated young naturalists of his generation. He was not a reformer, least of all a revolutionary; because of his own bitter poverty and his lifelong identification with the failures in American life, he yearned toward success with that love of the power-world that he was to confess in *The Financier* and *The Titan*. For all his reading in the complacently skeptical philosophers of late nineteenth-century materialism, he had no coherent philosophy and tended to brood like an animal in pain over the "welter" of life. When you compare him with the older realists, like Howells and Mark Twain, who were also challenged to their depths by the urbanized and plutocratic society of the nineties, and who were indeed outraged by its degradation of the old American freedom, you cannot help feeling that Dreiser was not even concerned with questions of human justice. These older writers had been formed by western life before the Civil War, with its relatively unformed class structure; egalitarianism was still the breath of life to them, as it had been to Whitman. They have an ethical directness (if no longer the old certainty), a deep sense of their own dignity, the artist's dignity, with all its consonant feeling for personal style, that are completely missing in Dreiser. Howells and Mark Twain are in their different ways elegiac in their hostility to the emerging new patterns of power; they were still outside the age they were writing in. Dreiser was not; he was confined to the American success story of the period for his whole experience of life.

The distinguishing quality of Dreiser's characters, that which particularly marks his thought as a novelist, is the air they have of being limited entirely to the society of their time, of being locked up in the terrible equation: life is only what America has made of it. His people are not simply *doomed,* like the characters in Frank Norris and John Dos Passos; the cards are not that coldly stacked against them. Dreiser is too little the prisoner even of his own theory, vague as it is, to fit his characters to a rule. It is rather that he can start only with what is most ordinary in life. He is possessed by the power of the banal. I think you would feel this even if you knew nothing about Dreiser's career. There is in *Sister Carrie* none of that savagery projected onto the eternal bourgeois which we find in Flaubert's portrait of Homais in *Madame Bovary,* or in Hemingway's ironically constructed platitudes. Far from being detached from "Sister" Carrie (whom he called that, unconsciously putting the name down on a piece of paper before he even thought of the novel, because she was *his* sister, as Jennie Gerhardt was another), he overvalues her symbolic humanity at the end of the book, addresses her sentimentally, does not seem to realize how mediocre she appears to us. These are the only kind of people he has ever known —the provincial girl on her way to the big city; the cheap drummer, Drouet; the flashy restaurant manager in Chicago, Hurstwood, with his rings and his condescending heartiness, whom the young Dreiser had so much envied. But in some way born of his own narrowness of experience, of his leaden concentration on what is most familiar to him, he brings us face to face with the idea of necessity.

If Dreiser were more sophisticated, more intellectually self-conscious, the effect of *Sister Carrie* would be diminished; we would feel that he is seeking to prove something to us, to give us a theory rather than an experience. And, in fact, Dreiser is very trying whenever he is tempted to "fine" writing—the difference between the careening "philosophy" of his chapter titles and the painfully sober prose of the narrative is startling. The chapter titles show Dreiser in his real uncertainty, trying to blow realism up into a metaphysic. But the awkward honesty of his narrative style is finally overwhelming; one feels the imponderable meanness of daily life.

Carrie looked about her, very much disturbed and quite sure that she did not want to work here. Aside from making her uncomfortable by sidelong glances, no one paid her the least attention. She waited until the whole department was aware of her presence. Then some word was sent around, and a foreman, in an apron and shirt sleeves, the latter rolled up to his shoulders, approached.

"Do you want to see me?" he asked.

"Do you need any help?" said Carrie, already learning directness of address.

"Do you know how to stitch caps?" he returned.

"No, sir," she replied.

"Have you ever had any experience at this kind of work?" he inquired.

She answered that she had not.

"Well," said the foreman, scratching his ear meditatively, "we do need a stitcher. We like experienced help, though. We've hardly got time to break people in." He paused and looked away out of the window. "We might, though, put you at finishing," he concluded reflectively.

"How much do you pay a week?" ventured Carrie, emboldened by a certain softness in the man's manner and his simplicity of address.

"Three and a half," he answered.

"Oh," she was about to exclaim, but checked herself and allowed her thoughts to die without expression.

"We're not exactly in need of anybody," he went on vaguely, looking her over as one would a package. "You can come on Monday morning, though," he added, "and I'll put you to work."

"Thank you," said Carrie weakly.

"If you come, bring an apron," he added.

He walked away, and left her standing by the elevator, never so much as inquiring her name.

The naiveté of this writing is oppressive; certainly nothing of its kind could be more clumsy than "Carrie, already learning directness of address," or less encouraging about a writer's mind than "she . . . allowed her thoughts to die without expression." Yet the whole scene, delivered in the most flat, toneless words, has in the context of Carrie's arrival in Chicago something heartbreaking about it. There is an immediate image of the factory wall itself, of what is purely abashed and helpless at this moment in Carrie, staring straight at it and at the man who spoke to her "vaguely, looking her over as one would a package." That "vaguely" makes the whole scene come through: Carrie is suspended in the inhuman air. I can never read it without a feeling of dread. And it is a dread that remains with me long after Carrie has made herself independent of factory jobs, since it is not to be explained by her joblessness alone. It is in the very nature of life. There is nothing else but this. We are moved not because these people are suffering—when they are, they cannot give voice to it—but because with these awkward gestures, these natural silences, these fits and starts and *ends* of communication (as if speech were the hopeless resumé of an experience too deep for it), they seem to be commenting uselessly on their own destinies.

The textbooks call it "determinism," and in its grimmest signification it is an idea which Dreiser upheld about as steadily as he did anything—that we are not responsible for what we do, that "we suffer for our temperaments, which we did not make, and for our weaknesses and lacks, which are no part of our willing or doing"—an idea which is anything but complacently "scientific," and in fact rouses us to a deeply felt sense of the mystery of the human condition, a compassion for all that is beyond our control. These people may not be conscious of the dark power that moves them; they may not protest; but they are humanity under the pressure of life itself; nothing intervenes between them and their destiny. There is an unconscious loneliness about them that is more affecting than any critical suffering could be, for *they do not know what is happening to them.* Carrie goes to Chicago, then to New York; she lives first with Drouet, then with Hurstwood; she becomes an actress and finally leaves Hurstwood, all with the same dreamy subjection to the forces around her. She is taken up, she plays a part, she is the unwitting instrument of Hurstwood's downfall; but fundamentally there is no reason for her doing one thing rather than another; she is simply swept on by accidents more akin to nature than to her nature; to the very end of the novel she takes in life with the same dim, incredulous stare with which she first looked on Chicago, a "lone figure in a tossing, thoughtless sea."

So, too, the deeper story in Hurstwood's degeneration is the general indifference to his fate. Once he has been cut off from his accustomed success in Chicago and has come, already more than half a failure, to New York, he is absolutely defenseless. He is falling out of life before our eyes; his decline is awful in its steady, remorseless consistency; there is no one—least of all

Carrie, the catalyst of his fate—to stop him. Yet worse than all this is the indifference, which he accepts as a matter of course and which really kills him. Force alone rules this world, as, Simone Weil has written, it ruled the world of the *Iliad*—a force like the tyranny of that everlasting war over the Homeric warriors for which the reasons have been almost forgotten, but which hangs over them like the real divinity that shapes life, calling out awe and submission in the heart of man. And it is our world, incontrovertibly it is *this* world, in its most naked essence. With all his faults, Dreiser has gone straight to the issue, that which it was his whole merit to understand—the tragedy of man in a society fundamentally more inhuman than "nature" ever was.

It is unnecessary here for me to speak at length of Dreiser's defects as an artist, of his fearful lapses in taste, of his pedestrianism—that which everyone knows best about him, and which has always made him fair game to his critics. At a time when his kind of writing is completely out of fashion, when we are ready—at most—to praise him for his "candor," to bury him deep among the pioneers of our self-conscious modern "honesty," it seems to me more useful to stress his involvement in the human problem, his creative pity, and all that this leads to in the actual texture of his novels—his way of converting his slowness, a certain stolidity in his world-view, into the novelist's grip on character. Dreiser certainly made every mistake a writer can make and still live; but in our current reaction against naturalism, we tend to forget that in his best work he is, fortunately, superior to his own ideas. For Dreiser was in many ways really an old-fashioned kind of realist, or "portrait-painter," with all that implies.

If, today, we do not go in for "solid" character, if we are suspicious—and rightly so—of his literalism, it is because we are not so stoutly sure of what character is. We see it as a complex of inward forces or symbols; it presses upon our consciousness as something half in and half out of the visible world we inhabit. We "have" a character only in its subtle infinitude of suggestion; but in all the flickerings there is the steadier light of an idea. Every note on a character is crossed by an intimation from the private imagination; in the merging, real voices are heard. For Dreiser, character was built up as a matter of course from the outward details—dress, the "brilliance" of the décor, the bourgeois details on which he feasted with such helpless admiration (how religiously he noted the splendor of the American parvenu in the big city!). And though some of the best things in his work are significantly moments of some deep human inarticulateness, of a half-felt awareness—Carrie facing the immensity of Chicago, Drouet coming upon Carrie in the dark, Hurstwood clinging to his rocker against life, Jennie Gerhardt following the body of her lover as the train bears his coffin out of the station—one remembers how methodically he got the surface toil of things into his books, piled up the "facts" until he forces the density of human affairs upon our minds. He was a man who could write, as it seems to us now, only from one end of the page to the other. His characters are so saturated in detail that long after they have withdrawn, their image is still blotted over the world through which they have passed.

Yet if they live so hauntingly for me, it is hardly because of Dreiser's literalism alone. It is because he still feels a certain awe before life as a whole; he was always amazed by what human beings do to each other. I do not think he ever explained naturalism very well by his excursions into philosophy and science, nor are we likely to forget the essential pathos of his career, which petered out after *An American Tragedy* into long years of silence, political confusion, and that fifth-rate work, *The Bulwark*. But for him character was still more than an instance of the social mechanism, a portion of the human tragedy. And it is in this that I mark the essential difference between Dreiser and the naturalists who come after him. For with them, as even Vernon Parrington had to admit (and Parrington was usually only too quick to honor a book just for its "liberal" message), the naturalistic novel relapses into social inquiry. There are the reformist tracts of Upton Sinclair, now largely unreadable except to students of the period, the work of a writer more radical than intelligent, and fundamentally not *radical* at all; there are the pseudo-Nietzschean adventure stories of Jack London; the documents of the Progressive period; the dreary wastes of the "proletarian" novel of the 1930s; the outraged war novelists, spewing up all the misery and degradation of war, but most of them hopelessly outweighed by one such cardinal work of imagination as E. E. Cummings' *The Enormous Room*; there is James T. Farrell, honest, eternally aggrieved, the very incarnation of all that was once so urgent and is now so mechanical in the American social novel.

Of late years Farrell has increasingly identified himself with Dreiser, and very understandably, for he comes out of much the same kind of world, he had the same long and bitter struggle against the arid Catholicism of his youth, and he has always written against all the obstacles that gentility and the rationalizations of "good taste" could put in his way. Yet creatively they seem to me quite different. For Farrell's real story—his only story—has been himself. Despite his militant defense of naturalism and the Marxist aura he has put around his novels, he has been unable to get free of his early struggles, much less to create characters out of his own imagination. He is much concerned today with defending the "tradition" of naturalism and has rather ambiguously found new ancestors for it, starting from Tolstoy and Chekhov. But this seems to have very little relevance to the actual spirit of his work; he tends to read into "naturalism" his own fierce ardors and defects as a writer. The truth is that his literary and political creed does not belong with the inner promptings of his novels. They are an autobiographical saga, the story of an education—deeply moving for what it tells us of his life, an unforgettable record of what society, behind its sleek and smiling face, has imposed upon the children of the "foreign" poor, especially when they are also heretics. But it is so repetitious and self-absorbed in its inspiration that to find ourselves being confronted these days with the same story in *Bernard Clare* and *The Road Between,* after the *Studs Lonigan* trilogy and the Danny O'Neill tetralogy, is to feel that Farrell has lost sight of the distinction between art and life.

The only naturalistic novelist in America after Dreiser who

seems to me interesting as an artist is John Dos Passos, a far more finished and expert writer, certainly, than Dreiser, and one whose inventive skill has influenced many European and American novelists. *U. S. A.* is inseparable from our consciousness of American life in the twentieth century. But I feel increasingly that it brings to an end a whole tradition of naturalistic social fiction in America, that it is the memorial not only to a vanished social period, but also to the kind of writing it embodies. I admire its inclusive power; I think I admire even more Dos Passos' feeling for the dissenters in American life against *all* the orthodoxies of the Left as well as of the Right. But somehow it is a very dated kind of book, wearisomely familiar; and this not because all the storms of our twentieth-century life play in it, but because it is too much like the thing it describes. It even seems to me quite a deadly book, conceived and carried through with a certain dead accuracy of contempt for most of the people in it.

I am not concerned here with Dos Passos' political opinions; so far as they are about the patterns of our society, I agree with them. The trend toward his current thought was implicit in *U. S. A.*; it has more and more directly entered into all his books since then, and it is of the very cast of his mind, skeptical, aloof, deeply alive to principles, concerned above all with the salvation of the individual in our mass society—and Dos Passos has always been on his side, no matter where he comes from. But the paradox of *U. S. A.* is that the individual does not get into it. What is the final effect of the fourfold plan—the narrative, the acrid "newsreels," the biographies of the true and false heroes of our time, the "Camera Eye" which is turned back on Dos Passos' own life—but to show man irrevocably split up between its mechanisms? And what is it that makes the "Camera Eye" section itself so ineffective and sentimental but that it is Dos Passos' only means of reflecting on the world he has created? It is the tiniest possible hole cut into the prison wall to let the spirit breathe. It is a confession that Dos Passos has closed himself up within his own devices.

In *U. S. A.* man is no longer part of history; he is only acted upon by forces, turned into a thing; and Dos Passos has not left himself time or space or love—certainly not Dreiser's brooding love—to plead for the people in it. The book is a triumph of method that confutes its moral purpose. Just as the narrative style has the final impersonality of a machine dragging lives into its maw, so the crucial images for the book, in its outward structure, its concrete details, are entirely functional and technological. In the end, Dos Passos is less compassionate for the victims than he is dazzled by the power mechanism that consumes them; he has created the greater machine. The book is an image of the *thing* that destroys almost everyone in it. It was the whole merit of naturalism to describe the society of our time, in its fundamental inhumanity; and here Dos Passos has done it almost too well; the artist has become like his subject. One cannot imagine Dos Passos going on from *U. S. A.* in the same spirit; and he has not. *U. S. A.* is uncomfortable proof—though evidence from even the young naturalists today is not lacking—that though naturalism brought us into the modern world, it has left us with the old problems demanding a new, a more specifically human, solution.

Contemporary American Literature in Its Relation to Ideas

> . . . Though no great minist'ring reason sorts
> Out the dark mysteries of human souls
> To clear conceiving: yet there ever rolls
> A vast idea before me, and I glean
> Therefrom my liberty . . .
>
> KEATS: *Sleep and Poetry*

THE question of the relation which should properly obtain between what we call creative literature and what we call ideas is a matter of insistent importance for modern criticism. It did not always make difficulties for the critic, and that it now makes so many is a fact which tells us much about our present relation to literature.

Ever since men began to think about poetry, they have conceived that there is a difference between the poet and the philosopher, a difference in method and in intention and in result. These differences I have no wish to deny. But a solidly established difference inevitably draws the fire of our question; it tempts us to inquire whether it is really essential or whether it is quite so settled and extreme as at first it seems. To this temptation I yield perhaps too easily, and very possibly as the result of an impercipience on my part—it may be that I see the difference with insufficient sharpness because I do not have a proper

NOTE. This essay is copyright 1949 by Lionel Trilling. Under the title "The Meaning of a Literary Idea" it is published also in Mr. Trilling's *The Liberal Imagination* (New York: Viking, 1950), and a slightly different version appeared in the *American Quarterly* (Fall 1949) under the title used here.

notion either of the matter of poetry or of the matter of philosophy. But whatever the reason, when I consider the respective products of the poetic and of the philosophic mind, although I see that they are by no means the same and although I can conceive that different processes, even different mental faculties, were at work to make them and to make them different, I cannot resist the impulse to put stress on their similarity and on their easy assimilation to each other.

Let me suggest some of the ways in which literature, by its very nature, is involved with ideas. I can be quite brief because what I say will not be new to you.

The most elementary thing to observe is that literature is of its nature involved with ideas because it deals with man in society, which is to say that it deals with formulations, valuations, and decisions, some of them implicit, others explicit. Every sentient organism *acts* on the principle that pleasure is to be preferred to pain, but man is the sole creature who formulates or exemplifies this as an idea and causes it to lead to other ideas. His consciousness of self abstracts this principle of action from his behavior and makes it the beginning of a process of intellection or a matter for tears and laughter. And this is but one of the innumerable assumptions or ideas that are the very stuff of literature.

This is self-evident and no one ever thinks of denying it. All that is ever denied is that literature is within its proper function in bringing these ideas to explicit consciousness, or ever gains by doing so. Thus, one of the matters of assumption in any society is the worth of men as compared with the worth of women; upon just such an assumption, more or less settled, much of the action of the *Oresteia* is based and we don't in the least question the propriety of this—or not until it becomes the subject of open debate between Apollo and Athene, who, on the basis of an elaborate biological speculation, try to decide which is the less culpable, to kill your father or to kill your mother. At this point we, in our modern way, feel that in permitting the debate Aeschylus has made a great and rather silly mistake, that he has for the moment ceased to be *literary*. Yet what drama does not consist of the opposition of formulable ideas, what drama, indeed, is not likely to break into the explicit exposition and debate of these ideas?

This, as I say, is elementary. And scarcely less elementary is the observation that whenever we put two emotions into juxtaposition we have what we can properly call an idea. When Keats brings together, as he so often does, his emotions about love and his emotions about death, we have a very powerful idea and the source of consequent ideas. The force of such an idea depends upon the force of the two emotions which are brought to confront each other, and also, of course, upon the way the confrontation is contrived.

Then it can be said that the very form of a literary work, considered apart from its content, so far as that is possible, is in itself an idea. Whether we deal with syllogisms or poems, we deal with dialectic—with, that is, a developing series of statements. Or if the word *statements* seems to prejudge the question so far as literature is concerned, let us say merely that we deal with a developing series—the important word is *developing*. We judge the value of the development by judging the interest of its several stages and the propriety and the relevance of their connection among themselves. We make the judgment in terms of the implied purpose of the developing series.

Dialectic, in this sense, is just another word for form, and has for its purpose, in philosophy or in art, the leading of the mind to some conclusion. Greek drama, for example, is an arrangement of moral and emotional elements in such a way as to conduct the mind—"inevitably," as we like to say—to a certain affective condition. This condition is a quality of personal being which may be judged by the action it can be thought ultimately to lead to.

We take Aristotle to be a better critic of the drama than Plato because we perceive that Aristotle understood and Plato did not understand that the form of the drama was of itself an idea which controlled and brought to a particular issue the subordinate ideas it contained. The form of the drama *is* its idea, and its idea *is* its form. And form in those arts which we call abstract is no less an idea than is form in the representational arts. Governments nowadays are very simple and accurate in their perception of this—much more simple and accurate than are academic critics and estheticians—and they are as quick to deal with the arts of "pure" form as they are to deal with ideas stated in discourse: it is as if totalitarian governments kept in mind what the rest of us tend to forget, that *idea* in one of its early significations exactly means form and was so used by many philosophers.

It is helpful to have this meaning before us when we come to consider that particular connection between literature and ideas which presents us with the greatest difficulty, the connection that involves highly elaborated ideas, or ideas as we have them in highly elaborated systems such as philosophy, or theology, or science. The modern feeling about this relationship is defined by two texts, both provided by T. S. Eliot. In his essay on Shakespeare Mr. Eliot says, "I can see no reason for believing that either Dante or Shakespeare did any thinking on his own. The people who think that Shakespeare thought are always people who are not engaged in writing poetry, but who are engaged in thinking, and we all like to think that great men were like ourselves." And in his essay on Henry James Mr. Eliot makes the well-known remark that James had a mind so fine that no idea could violate it.

In both statements, I believe, Mr. Eliot permits his impulse to spirited phrase to run away with him, yielding too much to what he conceives to be the didactic necessities of the moment, for he has it in mind to offer resistance to the nineteenth-century way of looking at poetry as a heuristic medium, as a communication of knowledge. This is a view which is well exemplified in a sentence of Carlyle's: "If called to define Shakespeare's faculty, I should say superiority of Intellect, and think that I had included all in that." As between the two statements about Shakespeare's mental processes, I give my suffrage to Carlyle's as representing a more intelligible and a more available notion of intellect than Mr. Eliot's, but I think I understand what Mr. Eliot is trying to do with his—he is trying to rescue poetry from the kind of misinterpretation of Carlyle's view which was once more common than it is now; he is trying to save for poetry what is peculiar to it, and for systematic thought what is peculiar to it.

As for Mr. Eliot's statement about James and ideas, it is useful to us because it gives us a clue to what might be called the sociology of our question. "Henry James had a mind so fine that no idea could violate it." In the context *violate* is a strong word, yet we can grant that the mind of the poet is a sort of Clarissa Harlowe and that an idea is a sort of Colonel Lovelace, for it is a truism of contemporary thought that the whole nature of man is in danger of being brutalized by the intellect, or at least by some of its apparently accredited surrogates. A specter haunts our culture—it is that people will eventually be unable to say, "They fell in love and married," let alone understand the language of *Romeo and Juliet,* but will as a matter of course say, "Their libidinal impulses being reciprocal, they activated their individual erotic drives and integrated them within the same frame of reference."

Now this is not the language of abstract thought or of any kind of thought. It is the language of non-thought. But it is the language which is developing from the peculiar status which we in our culture have given to abstract thought. There can be no doubt whatever that it constitutes a threat to the emotions and thus to life itself.

The specter of what this sort of language suggests has haunted us since the end of the eighteenth century. When he speaks of the mind being violated by an idea, Mr. Eliot, like the romantics, is simply voicing his horror at the prospect of life being intellectualized out of all spontaneity and reality.

We are the people of the idea, and we rightly fear that the intellect will dry up the blood in our veins and wholly check the emotional and creative part of the mind. And although I said that the fear of the total sovereignty of the abstract intellect be-

gan in the romantic period, we are of course touching here upon
Pascal's opposition between two faculties of the mind, of which
l'esprit de finesse has its heuristic powers no less than *l'esprit de
géométrie,* powers of discovery and knowledge which have a
particular value for the establishment of man in society and the
universe.

But to call ourselves the people of the idea is to flatter ourselves. We are rather the people of ideology, which is a very different thing. Ideology is not the product of thought; it is the
habit or the ritual of showing respect for certain formulas to
which, for various reasons having to do with emotional safety,
we have very strong ties but of whose meaning and consequences
in actuality we have no clear understanding. The nature of
ideology may in part be understood from its tendency to develop
the sort of language I parodied, and scarcely parodied, a moment
ago.

It is therefore no wonder that any critical theory that conceives itself to be at the service of the emotions, and of life
itself, should turn a very strict and jealous gaze upon an intimate relationship between literature and ideas, for in our culture
ideas tend to deteriorate into ideology. And indeed it is scarcely
surprising that criticism, in its zeal to protect literature and life
from the tyranny of the rational intellect, should misinterpret
the relationship. Mr. Eliot, if we take him literally, does indeed
misinterpret the relationship when he conceives of "thinking"
in such a way that it must be denied to Shakespeare and Dante.
It must puzzle us to know what thinking is if Shakespeare and
Dante did not do it.

And it puzzles us to know what René Wellek and Austin
Warren mean when in their admirable *Theory of Literature* they
say that literature can make use of ideas only when ideas "cease
to be ideas in the ordinary sense of concepts and become symbols, or even myths." I am not sure that the ordinary sense of
"ideas" actually is "concepts," or at any rate concepts of such
abstractness that they do not arouse in us feelings and attitudes.
And I take it that when we speak of the relationship of literature

and ideas, the ideas we refer to are not those of mathematics or of symbolic logic, but only such ideas as can arouse and traditionally have aroused the feelings—the ideas, for example, of men's relation to each other and to the world.

A poet's simple statement of a psychological fact recalls us to a proper simplicity about the nature of ideas. "Our continued influxes of feeling," said Wordsworth, "are modified and directed by our thoughts, which are indeed the representatives of all our past feelings." The interflow between emotion and idea is a psychological fact which we do well to keep clearly in mind, together with the part that is played by desire, will, and imagination in philosophy as well as in literature. Mr. Eliot, and Mr. Wellek and Mr. Warren—and in general those critics who are zealous in the defense of the autonomy of poetry—prefer to forget the ground which is common to both emotion and thought; they presume ideas to be only the product of formal systems of philosophy, not remembering, at least on the occasion of their argument, that poets too have their effect in the world of thought. *L'esprit de finesse* is certainly not to be confused with *l'esprit de géométrie,* but neither—which is precisely the point of Pascal's having distinguished and named the two different qualities of mind—is it to be denied its powers of comprehension and formulation.

Mr. Wellek and Mr. Warren tell us that "the artist will be hampered by too much ideology if it remains unassimilated."[1] We note the tautology of the statement—for what else is "too much" ideology except ideology that *is* unassimilated?—not because we wish to take a disputatious advantage over authors to whom we have reason to be grateful, but because the tautology suggests the uneasiness of the position it defends. We are speaking of art, which is an activity that defines itself exactly by its powers of assimilation and of which the essence is the just amount of any of its qualities or elements; of course too much or unassimilated ideology will "hamper" the artist, but so will too much of anything, so will too much metaphor: Coleridge tells us that in a long poem there can be too much *poetry*. The theoretical question is simply being begged, out of an undue anxiety over the "purity" of literature, over its perfect literariness.

The authors of *Theory of Literature* are certainly right to question the "intellectualist misunderstanding of art" and the "confusions of the functions of art and philosophy" and to look for the flaws in the scholarly procedures which organize works of art according to their ideas and their affinities with philosophical systems. Yet on their own showing there has been a conscious commerce between the poet and the philosopher, and not every poet has been violated by the ideas that have attracted him. The sexual metaphor is forced upon us, not only explicitly by Mr. Eliot but also implicitly by Mr. Wellek and Mr. Warren, who seem to think of ideas as masculine and gross and of art as feminine and pure, and who permit a union of the two sexes only when ideas give up their masculine, effective nature and "cease to be ideas in the ordinary sense and become symbols, or even myths." We naturally ask: symbols of what, myths about what? No anxious exercise of esthetic theory can make the ideas of, say, Blake and Lawrence other than what they are intended to be—ideas relating to action and to moral judgment.

This anxiety lest the work of art be other than totally self-contained, this fear lest the reader make reference to something beyond the work itself, has its origin, as I have previously suggested, in the reaction from the earlier impulse—it goes far back beyond the nineteenth century—to show that art is justified in comparison with the effective activity of the systematic disciplines. It arises too from the strong contemporary wish to establish, in a world of unremitting action and effectiveness, the legitimacy of contemplation, which it is now no longer convenient to associate with the exercises of religion but which may be associated with the experiences of art. We will all do well to advance the cause of contemplation, to insist on the right to a haven from perpetual action and effectiveness. But we must not enforce our insistence by dealing with art as if it were a unitary thing, and by making reference only to its "purely" esthetic element, requiring that every work of art serve our contemplation by being wholly self-contained and without relation to action.

No doubt there is a large body of literature to which ideas, with their tendency to refer to action and effectiveness, are alien and inappropriate. But also much of literature wishes to give the sensations and to win the responses that are given and won by ideas, and it makes use of ideas to gain its effects, considering ideas—like people, sentiments, things, and scenes—to be indispensable elements of human life. Nor is the intention of this part of literature always an esthetic one in the strict sense that Mr. Wellek and Mr. Warren have in mind; there is abundant evidence that the esthetic upon which the critic sets primary store is to the poet himself frequently of only secondary importance.

We can grant that the province of poetry is one thing and the province of intellection another. But keeping the difference well in mind, we must yet see that systems of ideas have a particular quality which is much coveted as their chief effect—let us even say as their chief esthetic effect—by at least certain kinds of literary works. Say what we will as critics and teachers trying to defend the province of art from the dogged tendency of our time to ideologize all things into grayness, say what we will about the "purely" literary, the purely esthetic values, we as readers know that we demand of our literature some of the virtues which define a successful work of systematic thought. We want it to have—at least when it is appropriate for it to have, which is by no means infrequently—the authority, the cogency, the completeness, the brilliance, the *hardness* of systematic thought.[2]

Of late years criticism has been much concerned to insist on the indirection and the symbolism of the language of poetry. I do not doubt that the language of poetry is very largely that of indirection and symbolism. But it is not only that. Poetry is closer to rhetoric than we today are willing to admit; syntax plays a greater part in it than our current theory grants, and syntax connects poetry with rational thought, for, as Hegel says, "grammar, in its extended and consistent form"—by which he means syntax—"is the work of thought, which makes its categories distinctly visible therein." And those poets of our time who make the greatest impress upon us are those who are most aware of rhetoric, which is to say of the intellectual content of their work. Nor is the intellectual content of their work simply the inevitable effect produced by good intelligence turned to poetry; many of these poets—Yeats and Eliot himself come most immediately to mind—have been at great pains to develop consistent intellectual positions along with, and consonant with, their work in poetry.

The esthetic effect of intellectual cogency, I am convinced, is not to be slighted. Let me give an example for what it is worth. Of recent weeks my mind has been much engaged by two statements, disparate in length and in genre, although as it happens they have related themes. One is a couplet of Yeats:

> We had fed the heart on fantasies,
> The heart's grown brutal from the fare.

I am hard put to account for the force of the statement. It certainly does not lie in any metaphor, for only the dimmest sort of metaphor is to be detected. Nor does it lie in any special power of the verse. The statement has for me the pleasure of relevance and cogency, in part conveyed to me by the content, in part by the rhetoric. The other statement is Freud's short book, his last, *An Outline of Psychoanalysis,* which gives me a pleasure which is no doubt different from that given by Yeats' couplet, but which is also similar; it is the pleasure of listening to a strong, decisive, self-limiting voice uttering statements to which I can give assent. The pleasure I have in responding to Freud I find very difficult to distinguish from the pleasure which is involved in responding to a satisfactory work of art.

Intellectual assent in literature is not quite the same thing as agreement. We can take pleasure in literature where we do not agree, responding to the power or grace of a mind without admitting the rightness of its intention or conclusion—we can take our pleasure from an intellect's *cogency*, without making a final judgment on the correctness or adaptability of what it says.

And now I leave these general theoretical matters for a more particular concern—the relation of contemporary American literature to ideas. In order to come at this as directly as possible we might compare modern American prose literature—for American poetry is a different thing—with modern European literature. European literature of, say, the last thirty or forty years seems to me to be, in the sense in which I shall use the word, essentially an active literature. It does not, at its best, consent to be merely comprehended. It refuses to be understood as a "symptom" of its society, although of course it may be that, among other things. It does not submit to being taped. We as scholars and critics try to discover the source of its effective energy and of course we succeed in some degree. But inevitably we become aware that it happily exists beyond our powers of explanation, although not, certainly, beyond our powers of response. Proust, Joyce, Lawrence, Kafka, and Eliot himself do not allow us to finish with them; and the refusal is repeated by a great many European writers less large than these.

With exceptions that I shall note, the same thing cannot be said of modern American literature. American literature seems to me essentially passive: our minds tend always to be made up about this or that American author, and we incline to speak of him, not merely incidentally but conclusively, in terms of his moment in history, of the conditions of the culture that "produced" him. Thus American literature as an academic subject is not so much a *subject* as an *object* of study; it does not, as a literature should, put the scrutinizer of it under scrutiny but, instead, leaves its students with a too comfortable sense of complete comprehension.

When we try to discover the root of this difference between European and American literature, we are led to the conclusion that it is the difference between the number and weight or force of the ideas which the two literatures embody or suggest. I do not mean that European literature makes use of, as American literature does not, the ideas of philosophy or theology or science. Kafka does not exemplify Kierkegaard, Proust does not dramatize Bergson. One way of putting the relationship of this literature to ideas is to say that the literature of contemporary Europe is in competition with philosophy, theology, and science, that it seeks to match them in comprehensiveness and power and seriousness.

This is not to say that the best of contemporary European literature makes upon us the effect of a rational system of thought. Quite the contrary, indeed; it is precisely its artistic power that we respond to, which I take in part to be its power of absorbing and disturbing us in secret ways. But this power it surely derives from its commerce, according to its own rules, with systematic ideas.

For in the great issues with which the mind has traditionally been concerned there is, I would submit, something *primitive* which is of the highest value to the literary artist. I know that it must seem a strange thing to say, for we are in the habit of thinking of systematic ideas as being of the very essence of the nonprimitive, of the highly developed. No doubt they are, but they are at the same time the means by which a complex civilization keeps the primitive in mind and refers to it. Whence and whither, birth and death, fate, free will, and immortality—these are never far from systematic thought; and Freud's belief that the child's first inquiry (beyond which, really, the adult does not go in kind) is in effect a sexual one seems to me to have an empirical support from literature. The ultimate questions of conscious and rational thought about the nature of man and his destiny match easily in the literary mind with the dark *unconscious* and with the most primitive human relationships. Love, parenthood, incest, patricide: these are what the great ideas suggest to literature, these are the means by which they express themselves. I need but mention three great works of different ages to suggest how true this is: *Oedipus, Hamlet, The Brothers Karamazov.*

Ideas, if they are large enough and of a certain kind, not only are not hostile to the creative process, as some think, but are virtually inevitable to it. Intellectual power and emotional power go together. And if we can say, as I think we can, that contemporary American prose literature in general lacks emotional power, it is possible to explain the deficiency by reference to the intellectual weakness of American prose literature.

The situation in verse is different. Perhaps this may be accounted for by the fact that the best of our poets are, as good poets usually are, scholars of their tradition. There is present to their minds the degree of intellectual power which poetry is traditionally expected to exert. Questions of form and questions of language seem of themselves to demand, or to create, an adequate subject matter; and a highly developed esthetic implies a matter strong enough to support its energy. We have not a few poets who are subjects and not objects, who are active and not passive. One does not finish quickly, if at all, with the best work of, say, Cummings, Stevens, and Marianne Moore. This work is not exempt from our judgment, even from adverse judgment, but it is able to stay with a mature reader as a continuing element of his spiritual life. Of how many writers of prose fiction can we say anything like the same thing?

The topic which was originally proposed to me and which I have taken the liberty of generalizing was the debt of four American writers to Freud and Spengler. The four writers were O'Neill, Dos Passos, Wolfe, and Faulkner. Of the first three how many can be continuing effective elements of our mental lives? I hope I shall never read Mr. Dos Passos without interest nor ever lose the warm though qualified respect that I feel for his work. But it is impossible for me to feel of this work that it is autonomous, that it goes on existing beyond our powers of explanation. As for Eugene O'Neill and Thomas Wolfe, I can respect the earnestness of their dedication, but I cannot think of having a living, reciprocal relation with what they have written. And I believe the reason is that these men, without intellectual capital of their own, don't owe a sufficient debt of ideas to anyone.

Spengler is certainly not a great mind; at best he is but a considerable dramatist of the idea of world history and of, as it were, the natural history of cultures; and we can find him useful as a critic who summarizes the adverse views of our urban, naturalistic culture which many have held. Freud is a very great mind indeed. Without stopping to specify what actual influence of ideas was exerted by Spengler and Freud on O'Neill, Dos Passos, or Wolfe or even to consider whether there was any influence at all, we can fairly assume that all are in something of the same ambiance. But if, in that ambiance, we want the sense of the actuality of doom—actuality being one of the qualities we expect of literature—surely we do better to seek it in Spengler himself than in any of the three literary artists, just as, if we want the sense of the human mystery, of tragedy truly conceived in the great terms of free will, necessity, and hope, surely we do far better to seek it directly in Freud himself than in these three literary men.

In any extended work of literature, the esthetic effect, as I have said, depends in large degree upon intellectual power, upon the amount and recalcitrance of the material the mind works on, and upon the mind's success in mastering the tough material. And it is exactly the lack of intellectual power that makes our three writers, after our first response of interest, so inadequate esthetically. We have only to compare, for example, Dos Passos' *U. S. A.* to a work of similar kind and intention, Flaubert's *L'Education Sentimentale,* to see that in Dos Passos' novel the matter encompassed is both less in amount and less in resistance than in Flaubert's; the energy of the encompassing mind is also less. Or we consider O'Neill's crude, dull notion of the unconscious and his merely elementary grasp of Freud's ideas about sex and we recognize the lamentable signs of a general inadequacy of mind.

Or we ask what it is about Thomas Wolfe that always makes us uncomfortable with his talent, so that even his admirers deal with him not as a subject but as an object—an object which must be explained and accounted for—and we are forced to answer that it is the disproportion between the energy of his utterance and his power of mind. It is customary to say of Thomas Wolfe that he is an emotional writer. Perhaps—although it is probably not the most accurate way to describe a writer who could deal with but one single emotion; and we feel that it is a function of his unrelenting, tortured egoism that he could not submit his mind to the ideas that might have brought the variety and interest of order to the single, dull chaos of his powerful self-regard, for it is true that the intellect makes many emotions out of the primary egoistic one.

At this point it may be well to recall what our subject is. It is not merely the part that is played in literature by those ideas which may be derived from the study of systematic, theoretical works; it is the part that is played in literature by ideas in general. To be sure, the extreme and most difficult instance of the general relation of literature to ideas is the relation of literature to highly developed and formulated ideas; and because this is indeed so difficult a matter, and one so often misconceived, I have put a special emphasis upon it. But we do not present our subject adequately—we do not, indeed, represent the mind adequately—if we think of ideas only as being highly formulated. It will bring us back to the proper generality of our subject if I say that the two contemporary writers who hold out to me the possibility of a living reciprocal relationship with their work are Ernest Hemingway and William Faulkner—it will bring us back the more dramatically because Hemingway and Faulkner have insisted on their indifference to the conscious intellectual tradition of our time and have acquired the reputation of achieving their effects by means that have the least possible connection with any sort of intellectuality or even with intelligence.

In trying to explain a certain commendable quality which is to be found in the work of Hemingway and Faulkner—and a certain quality only, not a total and unquestionable literary virtue—we are not called upon by our subject to show that particular recognizable ideas of a certain force or weight are "used" in the work. Nor are we called upon to show that new ideas of a certain force and weight are "produced" by the work. All that we need to do is account for a certain esthetic effect as being in some important part achieved by a mental process which is not different from the process by which discursive ideas are conceived, and which is to be judged by some of the criteria by which an idea is judged.

The esthetic effect which I have in mind can be suggested by a word I have used before—activity. We feel that Hemingway and Faulkner are intensely at work upon the recalcitrant stuff of life; when they are at their best they give us the sense that the amount and intensity of their activity are in a satisfying proportion to the recalcitrance of the material. And our pleasure in their activity is made the more secure because we have the distinct impression that the two novelists are not under any illusion that they have conquered the material upon which they direct their activity. The opposite is true of Dos Passos, O'Neill, and Wolfe; at each point of conclusion in their work we feel that *they* feel they have said the last word, and we feel this even when they represent themselves, as O'Neill and Wolfe so often do, as puzzled and baffled by life. But of Hemingway and Faulkner we seldom have the sense that they have deceived themselves, that they have misrepresented to themselves the nature and the difficulty of the matter they work on. And we go on to make another intellectual judgment: we say that the matter they present, together with the degree of difficulty which they assume it to have, seems to be very cogent. This, we say, is to the point; this really has something to do with life as we live it; we cannot ignore it.

There is a traditional and aggressive rationalism that can understand thought only in its conscious, developed form and believes that the phrase *unconscious mind* is a meaningless contradiction in terms. Such a view, wrong as I think it is, has at least the usefulness of warning us that we must not call by the name of thought or idea all responses of the human organism whatever. But the extreme rationalist position ignores the simple fact that the life of reason, at least in its most extensive part, begins in the emotions. What comes into being when two contradictory emotions are made to confront each other and are required to have a relationship with each other is, as I have said, quite properly called an idea. Ideas may also be said to be generated in the opposition of ideals, and in the felt awareness of the impact of new circumstances upon old forms of feeling and estimation, in the response to the conflict between new exigencies and old pieties. And it can be said that a work will have what I have been calling cogency in the degree that the confronting emotions go deep, or in the degree that the old pieties are firmly held and the new exigencies strongly apprehended.

In Hemingway's stories[3] a strongly charged piety toward the ideals and attachments of boyhood and the lusts of maturity is in conflict not only with the imagination of death but also with that imagination as it is peculiarly modified by the dark negation of the modern world. Faulkner as a southerner of today, a man deeply implicated in the pieties of his tradition, is of course at the very heart of an exigent historical event which thrusts upon him the awareness of the inadequacy and wrongness of the very tradition he loves. In the work of both men the cogency is a function not of their conscious but of their unconscious minds. We can, if we admire Tolstoy and Dostoevski, regret the deficiency of consciousness, blaming it for the inadequacy in both our American writers of the talent for generalization.[4] Yet it is to be remarked that the unconscious minds of both men have wisdom and humility about themselves. They seldom make the attempt at formulated solution, they rest content with the "negative capability." And this negative capability, this willingness to remain in uncertainties, mysteries, and doubts, is not, as one tendency of modern feeling would suppose, an abdication of intellectual activity. Quite to the contrary, it is precisely an aspect of their intelligence, of their seeing the full force and complexity of their subject matter. And this we can understand the better when we observe how the unconscious minds of Dos Passos, O'Neill, and Wolfe do not possess humility and wisdom; nor are they fully active, as the intellectual histories of all three men show.

A passivity on the part of Dos Passos before the idea of the total corruption of American civilization has issued in his recent denial of the possibility of economic and social reform and in his virtually unqualified acceptance of the American status quo. A passivity on the part of O'Neill before the clichés of economic and metaphysical materialism issued in his later simplistic Catholicism. The passivity of Thomas Wolfe before all his experience led him to that characteristic malice toward the objects or partners of his experience which no admirer of his ever takes account of, and eventually to that simple affirmation, recorded in *You Can't Go Home Again,* that literature must become the agent of the immediate solution of all social problems and undertake the prompt eradication of human pain; and because his closest friend did not agree that this was a possible thing for literature to do, Wolfe terminated the friendship. These are men of whom it is proper to speak of their having been violated by ideas; but we must observe that it was an excess of intellectual passivity that invited the violence.

In speaking of Hemingway and Faulkner I have used the word *piety*. It is a word that I have chosen with some care and despite the pejorative meanings that nowadays adhere to it, for I wished to avoid the word *religion,* and piety is not religion, yet I wished to have religion come to mind as it inevitably must when piety is mentioned. Carlyle says of Shakespeare that he was the product of medieval Catholicism and implies that Catholicism *at the distance at which Shakespeare stood from it* had much to do with the power of Shakespeare's intellect. Allen Tate has developed in a more particular way an idea that has much in common with what Carlyle here implies. Loosely put, the idea is that religion in its decline leaves a detritus of pieties, of strong assumptions, which afford a particularly fortunate condition for certain kinds of literature; these pieties carry a strong charge of intellect, or perhaps it would be more accurate to say that they tend to stimulate the mind in a powerful way.

Religious emotions are singularly absent from Shakespeare and it does not seem possible to say of him that he was a religious man. Nor does it seem possible to say of the men of the great period of American literature in the nineteenth century that they were religious men. Hawthorne and Melville, for example, lived at a time when religion was in decline and they were not drawn to support it. But from religion they inherited a body of pieties, a body of issues, if you will, which engaged their hearts and their minds to the very bottom. Henry James was not a religious man and there is not the least point in the world in trying to make him out one. But you need not accept all the implications of Quentin Anderson's thesis that James allegorized his father's religious system to see that Mr. Anderson is right when he says that James was dealing, in his own way, with the questions that his father's system propounded. This will indicate something of why James so catches our imagination today, and why we turn so eagerly again to Hawthorne and Melville.

The piety which descends from religion is not the only possible piety, as the case of Faulkner reminds us, and perhaps also the case of Hemingway. But we naturally mention first that piety which does descend from religion because it is most likely to have in it the quality of transcendence which, whether we admit it or no, we expect literature at its best to have.

The subject is extremely delicate and complex and I do no more than state it barely and crudely. But no matter how I state it, I am sure you will see that what I am talking about leads us to the crucial issue of our literary culture.

Perhaps I may assume that most of us are in our social and political beliefs consciously liberal and democratic. Probably most of us, in the degree of our commitment to literature and our familiarity with it, find that the contemporary authors we most wish to read and most wish to admire for their literary qualities demand of us a great agility and ingenuity in coping with their antagonism to our social and political ideals. For it is in general true that the modern European literature with which we can have an active, reciprocal relationship—the right relationship to have—has been written by men who are indifferent to or even hostile to the tradition of democratic liberalism as we know it. Yeats and Eliot, Proust and Joyce, Lawrence and Gide —these men do not seem to confirm us in the social and political ideals which we hold.

If we now turn and consider the contemporary literature of America, we see that wherever we can describe it as patently liberal and democratic, we must say that it is not of lasting interest. I do not say that the work which is written to conform to the liberal democratic tradition is of no value but only that we do not incline to return to it, we do not establish it in our minds and affections. Very likely we learn from it as citizens; and as citizen-scholars and citizen-critics we understand and explain it. But we do not live in an active reciprocal relation with it. The sense of largeness, of cogency, of the transcendence which largeness and cogency can give, the sense of being reached in our secret and primitive minds—this we virtually never get from the writers of the liberal democratic tradition at the present time.

And since liberal democracy inevitably generates a body of ideas, it must necessarily occur to us to ask why it is that these particular ideas have not infused with force and cogency the literature that embodies them. This question is the most important, the most fully challenging question in culture that at this moment we can ask.

The answer to it cannot of course even be begun here, and I shall be more than content if it now is merely accepted as a legitimate question. But there are one or two things that may be said about the answer, about the direction we must take to reach it in its proper form. We will not find it if we come to facile conclusions about the absence from our culture of the impressive ideas of traditional religion. I have myself referred to the historical fact that religion has been an effective means of transmitting or of generating ideas of a sort which I feel are necessary for the literary qualities we want, and to some this will no doubt mean that I believe religion to be a necessary condition of great literature. I do not believe that; and what is more, I consider it from many points of view an impropriety to try to guarantee literature by religious belief.

Nor will we find our answer if we look for it in the weaknesses of the liberal democratic ideas in themselves. It is by no means true that the inadequacy of the literature that connects itself with a body of ideas is a sign of the inadequacy of those ideas, although it is no doubt true that some ideas have less affinity with literature than others.

Our answer, I believe, will rather be found in a cultural fact— in the kind of relationship which we, or the writers who represent us, maintain toward the ideas we claim as ours, and in our habit of conceiving the nature of ideas in general. If we find it is true of ourselves that we conceive ideas to be pellets of intellection or crystallizations of thought, precise and completed, and defined by their coherence and their procedural recommendations, then we shall have accounted for the kind of prose literature we have. And if we find that we do indeed have this habit, and if we continue in it, we can predict that our literature will continue much as it is. But if we are drawn to revise our habit of conceiving ideas in this way and learn instead to think of ideas as living things, inescapably connected with our wills and desires, as susceptible of growth and development by their very nature, as showing their life by their tendency to change, as being liable, by this very tendency, to deteriorate and become corrupt and to work harm, then we shall stand in a relation to ideas which makes an active literature possible.

Notes

[1] The word *ideology* is used by Mr. Wellek and Mr. Warren not in the pejorative sense in which I have earlier used it but to mean simply a body of ideas.

[2] Mr. Wellek and Mr. Warren say something of the same sort, but only, as it were, in a concessive way: "Philosophy, ideological content, in its proper context, seems to enhance artistic value because it corroborates several important artistic values: those of complexity and coherence. . . . But it need not be so. The artist will be hampered by too much ideology if it remains un-

Lionel Trilling

assimilated" (p. 122). Earlier (p. 27) they say: "Serious art implies a view of life which can be stated in philosophical terms, even in terms of systems. Between artistic coherence . . . and philosophic coherence there is some kind of correlation." They then hasten to distinguish between emotion and thinking, sensibility and intellection, and the like, and to tell us that art is more complex than "propaganda."

[3] It is in the stories rather than in the novels that Hemingway is characteristic and at his best.

[4] Although there is more impulse to generalization than is usually supposed. This is especially true of Faulkner. who has never subscribed to the contemporary belief that only concrete words have power and that only the representation of things and actions is dramatic.

The American Poet in Relation to Science

IF this paper had been called "The American Poet and the Modern World," we should still be in very much the same position as when we discuss the problem of the American poet in relation to science. For we can hardly deny the fact that the world as we know it today is one whose physical reality has been defined by science. It has, one might guess, always been so. The poet, like anyone else who is honest about facts, must live in recognition of the physical world which surrounds him. He may ultimately go beyond it, but he must start from it. It is his *pied à terre*. If he has a difference from other men it does not lie in his being one of a race apart. The role of recorder of the new vistas comes to any Balboa who can be articulate after standing silent in wonder upon a peak in Darien. It was science which gave us the free world of the Renaissance and the apparent dignity and freedom of man. Again it is science which seems to have taken them from us, as we look out now in fear and trembling upon a new vista of knowledge.

Science with constant energy and exploration has provided us with a new topography of definitions. The world has not actually changed, but the description of it has widened and altered. The laws of Newton, the logic of Aristotle, and the geometry of Euclid no longer obtain except on the lowest level of habituated familiarity. The world as we are coming to see it today through the mind's eye of the scientist is no longer a substantive and regulated mechanics but a helter-skelter of electronics out of which we can extract for reliance only equations of infinite

154

variables. The path toward a demonstrable truth has become a maze of formulas whose following is no longer even a sport of kings, or if of kings it is a new sort. One can start hopefully with descriptive classifications but is led almost immediately into the mystery of functions. The search for the newest world has led into realms of space, energy, and changing matter. Man can describe his search with words, but even words, which have been our reliable source for the communication of experience, have been affected by science and are no longer valid in the positive referential sense to which we were accustomed.

At least one scientist has put the difficulty of communication bluntly, for more than his own profession. In a speech given in 1940, at the two hundredth anniversary of the founding of the University of Pennsylvania, Hermann Weyl, of the Institute for Advanced Study, had this to say about the present basis for communication:

Words are dangerous tools. Created for our everyday life they may have their good meanings under familiar limited circumstances, but Pete and the man in the street are inclined to extend them to wider spheres without bothering about whether they then still have a sure foothold in reality. We are witnesses of the disastrous effects of this witchcraft of words in the political sphere where all words have a much vaguer meaning, and human passion so often drowns the voice of reason. The scientist must thrust through the fog of abstract words to reach the concrete rock of reality.

This problem is not one for the scientist alone. Tripped up in fog on the concrete rock of physical reality, the poet can smash his head as thoroughly as the scientist can. Like political witches, the poet can become a fog-maker for others. The circumstances of the world are no longer familiar and limited. The poet has had to look upon a new physical reality and learn not to accept what has been thought about it simply because it has been thought. He has had to learn and devise a new vocabulary and syntax for giving extension to his conclusions. Old definitions of physical reality have lost validity. Old vocabularies have tottered. Their reference was to something which no longer exists in the same terms.

> Words strain,
> Crack and sometimes break, under the burden,
> Under the tension, slip, slide, perish,
> Decay with imprecision, will not stay in place,
> Will not stay still.[1]

This was T. S. Eliot in 1936 in his poem "Burnt Norton," the first of the *Four Quartets* where he has tried to present a harmony for man and the world. It is interesting and relevant that he has recently been a Fellow at the same Institute for Advanced Study of which Hermann Weyl is a member. There was a recognition of common ground in their appointments.

A poet, as craftsman, can begin only with words. He must know his medium. Eliot's attitude toward the instability of words was not an idiosyncracy. It was marked even more generally by the reasons for, and the effect of, Ogden and Richards' *The Meaning of Meaning*, which first appeared in 1923 and, although of the profoundest effect on modern poetic practice as well as its interpretation, was written by one man trained in psychology and another initially brought up as a mathematician. In later editions its supplementary essays were not by poets but by Malinowski, a cultural anthropologist, and by Crookshank, a doctor. The modern American poet's concern with words, with his medium, has at the very outset of his creative activity been profoundly affected by scientific thought. It is not fashion which causes him so often to talk about them. What was needed was a new dictionary.

The basic effect of science on the modern American poet has not been merely a matter of bringing over into verse the terminology of science or reference to its artifacts. This, of course, the poet has always done to some extent, though the pace of transmission has increased along with the broadening in general elementary education in science. This phase can be noted from the time of Whitman, with his

Hurrah for positive science! long live exact demonstration!

Whitman, nevertheless, was not basically interested in the abstract demonstrations of science, as he indicated in the scorn of his poem, "When I Heard the Learn'd Astronomer." What was exact for him was in terms of technological achievements—for example, in reference to science's development of the transcontinental railway, the Atlantic cable, and the engineering of the Suez Canal, which could unite the world by conquering distance and bring us on a Columbian passage to India. The poet could respond in terms of emotional quivering to the stimulus of an abstract demonstration of a formula, as Miss Millay in 1920 so popularly affirmed in

Euclid alone has looked on Beauty bare.[2]

This seems perhaps a step closer to apprehension of the scientific language of mathematics, but the expression of the sonnet itself veers from science; it is not only based on an already outmoded proposition but carries in its rhetoric nothing of scientific concept or discipline.

We can find more basic indications of the influence of scientific procedure on modes of poetic expression, as we retrace the poetic history of the last half-century. Certainly the most dominant personality of its first two decades was Ezra Pound, and its first group manifestation that of the Imagists. Theirs may seem to have been, in intent, poetry of pure distillation, as when H. D. describes heat or a pool, or when Pound pictures the scene "In a Station of the Metro." But if one re-examines Pound's and the Imagists' precepts, one can see something very much like an attempt at scientific precision, without value judgments, in the rendering of objects. "Direct treatment of the 'thing'," Pound says, "whether subjective or objective." "An 'Image' is that which presents an intellectual time and emotional complex in an instant of time. I use the term 'complex' rather in the technical sense employed by the newer psychologists . . ." "Use no superfluous word, no adjective, which does not reveal something."

Pound, by analogy, sounds like one of the seventeenth-century

Fellows of the Royal Society in their successful efforts to remove embellishment from diction in order to arrive at the point of scientific accuracy of description. Modern science had brought the consciousness also into its scope. What modern poets were after was, as Marianne Moore described it in a definition of poetry, "real toads in imaginary gardens," presented by "literalists of the imagination." This was a matter of starting from a punctiliously rendered actual world of stimulus. Its effect was to drive out of poetry the blurred fantasy of Kubla Khan's Xanadu which the romantic school had enjoyed in various forms, and to concentrate instead on a world which included as datum a piece of glass in a hospital yard or a red wheelbarrow shining in the sun. By the very generality of such data, this new method was a denial of the validity of any point of view which states that while some objects are suitable for poetry, others are not.

There is no hierarchy of values for the scientist in terms of the data he examines. The scientific attitude of modern man has reduced all material objects to a single level, or, if one prefers, raised all material objects upward together. Science has helped to teach and the poets have helped to demonstrate that all objects have an equal validity as the immediate subject of poetry, because all objects are similarly parts of the phenomenal world from which the reason and the imagination begin. As William Carlos Williams remarks, "The commonplace, the tawdry, the sordid all have their poetic uses if the imagination can lighten them. This broadening of the choice in the materials of poetry has great modern significance . . ." Williams knowingly denies his own categories. The tendency in modern poetry has been a greater realism.

This attempt on the part of the poet for greater realism of presentation has gone beyond the problem of rendering substantive matter. It includes the intangibles which science has disclosed. The poet may as yet comprehend little more than the mystery of the fourth dimension, yet he has understood that time as a concept is no longer chronological in the older definition but is without duration and is a state in which all things are coexistent. "In my beginning is my end," Mr. Eliot said in another section of the *Four Quartets*: "In the end is my beginning." "Keeping time," in his world, is a matter of an endless dance, of men as of colloids. It is good mysticism but it is also good science. Archibald MacLeish, in "You Andrew Marvell" (written in 1926) gives a fourth-dimensional version of that urgent time which had troubled the lover of a coy mistress three centuries before:

> And here face down beneath the sun
> And here upon earth's noonward height
> To feel the always coming on
> The always rising of the night[3]

In the passage just quoted from Mr. MacLeish there is not only an attempt at a precise rendering of the scientific concept of "time, space, curvature," but there is evidence of a new syntactical or structural arrangement of his words. There is in the poem really no proper subject or predicate, and there are no commas to break up a flow of data which passes endlessly through a constant present. The poem is at least in intent not simply a picture of what happens but the happening itself. One way of reducing the dichotomy between words and the things which they represent has been to make the words themselves things, and the structure of a poem itself an object. MacLeish has expressed this aim elsewhere, in the conclusion to his versified "Art of Poetry" (written in 1924):

> A poem should not mean
> But be[4]

There is no period to conclude either the poem or the statement of situation. It is motion and being. As the sculptor Gabo has said of his own medium: "A work of art is not the representation of an idea, it is itself the idea." This is again a twentieth-century kind of scientific realism.

Mr. MacLeish's poem is the simplest example of the way by which the modern poet has tried affirmatively to present the physical world which science has defined. It is an attempt to

The American Writer and the European Tradition

accommodate the physical data, as the scientist has tried to accommodate them through another variety of language. The scientist and the poet are not totally different. Willard Gibbs, perhaps the greatest speculative mind of the nineteenth century in America, is said to have retorted in a university faculty meeting which proposed the enhancement of modern languages over mathematics, "But, gentlemen, mathematics *is* a language!" He is said to have walked out of the room. Poets have come more and more to understand the scientist in other than the emotional response which Miss Millay gave to Euclid's theorem. Muriel Rukeyser, in the February 1949 issue of *Physics Today,* paid Gibbs and an aspect of modern science the tribute of a poet. "Willard Gibbs," she says,

is the type of the imagination at work in the world. His story is that of an opening-up which has had its effect on our lives and our thinking; and, it seems to me, it is the emblem of the naked imagination—which is called abstract and impractical, but whose discoveries can be used by anyone who is interested, in whatever "field"—an imagination which for me, more than that of any other figure in American thought, any poet, or political, or religious figure, stands for imagination at its essential points.

It is because he dealt in law and in relationships that one may come to him from any point of interest, however inadequate one's background be. I came to him through poetry, without any of the proper training, feeling that in this time, full of its silence in spite of the weight of paper and the weight of words poured on us every day, full of its barriers set up between the peoples of the world and any two people—in this time, our sources are to be reached. It seems to me that if we are in any way free, we are also free in relation to the past, and that we may to some extent choose our tradition.

This is how she describes his conclusions in a poem:

Laws are the gifts of their systems, and the man
in constant tension of experience drives
moments of coexistence into light.
It is the constitution of matter I must touch.
Deduction from deduction: entropy,

160

heat flowing down a gradient of nature,
perpetual glacier driving down the side
of the unknown world in an equilibrium tending
to uniformity, the single dream.
                                    He binds
himself to know the public life of systems.
Look through the wounds of law
at the composite face of the world.[5]

But despite the degree to which the poet has been able to accommodate the definitions of the scientist, the recent history of
American poetry shows a rift between the poet and the scientist.
It is difficult and perhaps unfair to define the scientist, for the
category includes not only the man in the laboratory but also an
Einstein or a Gibbs. Yet the familiar scientist has, if we may
generalize in terms of common homage, been concerned pre-
dominantly with physical reality and with consistent conclusions
which can be empirically demonstrated. He is, in such a role as
scientist, concerned only with description, classification, and abstraction, and not with qualities or values. He has conceived
knowledge as being confined within these limits. At least in his
professed technology he advances only inductively and rationally.
Science is at bottom always concerned with quantitative, meas-
urable things. Anything for which no yardstick is available is
under suspicion by the scientist. It is to this substantiality that
the average man has given his confidence. On this practicality
he has come more and more to lean.

The poet, on the other hand, having used the yardstick will
drop it to go beyond physics into metaphysics. He has accepted
as well a reality of the senses and of religious and ethical belief.
To physical reality he has added a reality of the imagination.
He has started from physics, but in reaching his conclusions he
has jumped ahead of his data on an essentially undemonstrable
and sometimes inconsistent procedure of intuition based on an
economy of the senses. It is true that the pure mathematician, in
practice, himself uses intuition and jumps ahead of his data to
a theorem to whose empirical substantiation he is indifferent. It

is for this reason that the imaginative world of the pure mathematician, with his self-consistent and "elegant" abstractions, lies close to the imaginative world of the poet. His equations are like metaphors to express insubstantialities. But in this very procedure the pure mathematician parts company with the mathematical physicist who, as more typical of the scientist, insists on empirical testing. Popular science has its separate path. Its pride is in rational induction.

This difference between definitions of reality, as well as in procedures for gaining useful knowledge, has distinguished the poet from the scientist and is the basis of a conflict characteristic of our time. The increased prestige of empirical science has seemed to wall out the poet. The poet, of course, has not actually remained outside the wall. He only denies the imposed restriction on vision and knowledge, and would put himself close to the pure mathematician whom he so much resembles. He thinks of the products of philosophy, pure mathematics, and poetry chiefly as variant metaphors for expressing what lies behind the phenomenal.

Wallace Stevens has said, in a speech before the English Institute in the autumn of 1948: "As for the present, what have we, if we do not have science, except the imagination. And who is to say of its deliberate fictions arising out of the contemporary mind that they are not forerunners of some such science." Scientific conformations of the fictions of the imagination may be determined by science. The poet, however, will, like the pure mathematician, be indifferent to the period of scientific proof required, if indeed scientific procedure can ever penetrate beyond the bounds of physical reality into the more inclusive sphere where the poet's imagination plays. The validity of the poet's conclusion need not be threatened. Physical reality endures, but only as partial reality. It must be acknowledged but not as dictator. The poet goes to it and then through it.

This relationship of physical reality to the area of the imagination is what so vitally modified Miss Moore's description of poetry as "real toads in imaginary gardens" and the poet as a "literalist of the imagination." The proper stresses fall on both "real" and "imaginary," on both "literalist" and "imagination." The poet's skill comes into play in his presentation of scientific knowledge, his daring as he penetrates through it into the imagination. In this latter realm, without having turned his back to anything but the self-imposed limits of physical science, he reaches what Stevens calls "the essential poem at the center of things." Like the equation, the poem within a poem will be self-consistent and "elegant" as an abstraction.

Such an answer is the poet's response to the "rage for order" in a world which has defined individual objects so precisely as to make the distinctions sharper than the relationships. It is his answer to apparent chaos. If the poet in response to the scientific destruction of the idea of a mechanical universe has filled the void by a procedural logic, he has done so with a new logic of intuition and the senses, in which coherence in chaos is obtained by the cohesive force of the imagination itself. When Hart Crane writes:

> There is the world dimensional for
> those untwisted by the love of things
> irreconcilable . . .[6]

he is counting on an ecstasy of the senses to reform and rebuild. When he writes in "Voyages II"

> And onward, as bells off San Salvador
> Salute the crocus lustres of the stars,
> In these poinsettia meadows of her tides,—
> Adagios of islands, O my Prodigal,
> Complete the dark confessions her veins spell [7]

one must know the modern scientific definition of the physical reality which he describes, but one must also be able, as he suggests, "to go *through* the combined materials of the poem," by a path he defines as a "logic of metaphor," into a coherent metaphysical reality. In Crane's poem this ultimate reality becomes a cool "Belle Isle." In Mr. Eliot's *Four Quartets* it is "at the still point of the turning world." The metaphors in poetry vary; the goal of modern poets is uniform.

The American Writer and the European Tradition

The "rage for order" is preceded by a rage for knowledge. Thus impelled, the scientist goes by the path of postulative data, that is, the situation in which the complete meaning of anything is known to be true only through precise logical and scientific description. Thus water becomes H_2O; and a pond is H_2O, with an index of refraction and a bottom composed of precisely named minerals with a certain weight per specific volume.

The modern poet's characteristic way of knowledge has been through concept by intuition, working toward a rendering of qualities. He knows that water in the form of rain is different from that in the form of a flood; and no knowledge derived simply from a scientific description will explain the realities of quenching thirst or destruction by flood. Therefore it has been his way to evoke the proper image and to learn from the image. If science took from the poet of our century a complete reliance on the individual meaning of words, the loss only served to emphasize to the poet the vital importance of the total image structured from a cluster of individual words, which gains its validity through ordered relationships. This is, it seems to me, what a man like Robert Frost meant when he said that "Metaphor is the whole of thinking." He was talking about the poet's way to the imagination and to the ultimate knowledge which man as poet desires.

In the hands of certain modern poets this conflict between science and poetry as ways to knowledge, or between procedures based solely on reason and those dependent also on intuition, has led to what appears to be an overt anti-intellectualism. We can find this in some of the poetry of a man like E. E. Cummings, who is quite aware of the fact that although the typographical arrangement of his poems is physically realistic, and to that degree "scientific," its primary impact and appeal are to the senses.

> since feeling is first
> who pays any attention
> to the syntax of things
> will never wholly kiss you . . .[8]

164

Cummings uses "syntax" pejoratively in the old fashion. He has constructed a new syntax, however, and pays attention to it. He has been influenced by scientific thought, but "feeling is first" for him as for most poets of the twentieth century. Eliot's way toward a metaphysics—though by the weight of his erudition it may seem an intellectual path—is, in his final period of waiting for illumination, intuitive and romantic. Physical reality has been taken into his account, and tradition and the individual talent explained in terms influenced by modern science. But "after such knowledge, what forgiveness?" The fulfilling knowledge of ultimate reality will come

> At the source of the longest river
> The voice of the hidden waterfall
> And the children in the apple-tree
> Not known, because not looked for
> But heard, half-heard, in the stillness
> Between two waves of the sea.[9]

Eliot's sea flows beyond the scientific reality of H_2O in which various mineral salts are dissolved. So, too, Hart Crane, having voyaged through the planes of his sea, found knowledge not in the consolation of a physical constitution of Belle Isle, but

> The imaged Word, it is, that holds
> Hushed willows anchored in its glow.
> It is the unbetrayable reply
> Whose accent no farewell can know.[10]

The poet, looking at the discoveries of science in relation to physical knowledge, has started from them and remembered them. But dissatisfied with the tendency of science to limit itself to physical reality alone, he has ventured beyond. He has constructed a jar in Tennessee which gives dominion to the wilderness. But the jar constructed by reason will be only "gray and bare" unless it can catch up in itself both bird and bush, and thus give true order as well as dominion. The values of the senses have been added to the technology of the reasonable potter. The final song by "One of Fictive Music" will be a physical jar and more than a jar. It will contain not only the "arrant spices" of the "physical sun" but the "other perfumes" of the metaphysical realm which bring the "difference" between sheer science and true poetry:

> Unreal, give back to us what once you gave:
> The imagination that we spurned and crave.[11]

This is an address to "unreality" only in the scientist's definition. Once regained, it is real enough.

Science has performed an inestimable service to modern poets in forcing them by a redefinition of physical reality to search out a revitalized manner of expression. The poetic diction and syntax of the past was worn out and exhausted. Science gave in her new terms a fresh beginning to poets. They served as challenges to poetical clichés. But science itself stopped short and was content with a limited view of reality confined to the empirical level only. So overwhelming was its revolution that it seemed self-sufficient. It developed a technology which became a comforting ritual for observance and endowed its own name with talismanic powers. Almost paradoxically it has become for the general run of man a pseudospiritual act of self-abnegation to creep into the tent of scientific procedure and knowledge, a place of substance but without values. The complexities and areas of technique and interlocking data have grown so great that the personality of the individual scientist has been lost to sight. The mathematical physicist has disappeared into his equation.

In a world which is unwilling to correlate the ways to knowledge of the scientist and poet, of reason and the imagination, the whole man has been lost by division. Personality is being erased as the area of reality is reduced. But if we look at the psychological history of twentieth-century America, it has been the poet, acting on the concept of intuition, still penetrating the mystery of both the physical and metaphysical as they affect himself as man, who has made the strongest public stand for the dignity and freedom of the individual. He has been the preserver of the Renaissance heritage. In his concept of total reality he has ac-

166

cepted what science has taught about this newest of new worlds, but in presenting it in a work of art he has made articulate an even wider sphere of discovery. It is at least possible that the American poet of the first half of the twentieth century may be the complete realist, though not necessarily the complete mirror of the temper of our age.

Notes

[1] T. S. Eliot, *Four Quartets* (New York: Harcourt, 1943) 7–8.

[2] *The Harp Weaver and Other Poems* (New York: Harper, 1923) 74. Copyright 1920–48 by Edna St. Vincent Millay.

[3] Archibald MacLeish, *Poems, 1924–1933* (Boston: Houghton, Mifflin, 1933) 58.

[4] *Ibid.*, 123.

[5] Muriel Rukeyser, *A Turning Wind* (New York: Viking, 1939) 97–98. Reprinted by permission of the author.

[6] Hart Crane, *The Collected Poems of Hart Crane* (New York: Liveright, 1933) 94.

[7] *Ibid.*, 102.

[8] E. E. Cummings, *Collected Poems* (New York: Harcourt, 1938) poem 180. Copyright 1926 by Horace Liveright.

[9] Eliot, *Four Quartets*, 39.

[10] Hart Crane, *Collected Poems*, 110.

[11] Wallace Stevens, "To the One of Fictive Music," *Harmonium* (New York: Knopf, 1931) 117.

Some European Views of Contemporary American Literature

OCCASION to see ourselves, not merely as others see us, but as they reflect our own reflection of ourselves, through whatever glass, however darkly—such is the hall of mirrors our subject opens before us. To traverse it, to glance in passing at its multiplied and refracted images, is not a proud but a chastening experience. Possibly it may lead us, via those corridors which our publicists are now contriving, into the midst of the American Century. Perhaps we can best comprehend the present vogue of American letters in Europe by remembering three brusque words used by Thomas Hobbes to account for the authority of the classics: "Colonies and Conquests." For, though we may well disclaim imperialistic or even commercial motives, we cannot disavow the situation that ties Western Europe to our country as no two continents have ever been tied before. Along with the Marshall Plan go jeeps and juke-boxes, CARE packages and foreign-language editions of the *Reader's Digest*; along with our products we export our culture—"culture" not in Matthew Arnold's terms but in Ruth Benedict's patterns. All this helps to explain what European critics can justify no better than we could: why the world's best seller, second only to the Bible, should be *Gone with the Wind*.

But this is the sort of tribute we cannot accept with much complacency. Culturally, even more than ideologically, we are unprepared for the role of hegemony that fortune seems determined to thrust upon us. Though we believe in our great literary tradition, we realize that its grandeur is far from Augustan. Its greatest works are so functionally adapted to the contours of the land itself that, in distant lands under different conditions, they may not serve as very usable models. Their characteristic virtues are critical, radical, pluralistic, exploratory—virtues which presuppose the settled existence of an older world. What Cooper did for Balzac or Emerson for Carlyle, what Poe did for Baudelaire or Whitman for Mayakovsky, what *Moby Dick* did for Lawrence of Arabia was to challenge that presupposition. In the past, precisely because Europe was central and America was tangential, European horizons were broadened by American minds. The flight of imagination toward the New World, the fantasy of Chateaubriand or Kafka, the nightmare of Dickens or Céline, was always centrifugal. In recent years, for better or worse, the center of international gravity has shifted. Strategic considerations have converted the U.S.A. from a place of escape to a place of retreat, from a source of exoticism to a source of recovery.

It is not surprising, therefore, that professors of English at Continental universities now convert themselves into professors of American; that brilliant European students take part in an American seminar at Salzburg; that major European periodicals are crowded with announcements and reviews of American books; that translation is consummated by imitation, the sincerest acknowledgment of cultural ascendancy. It is not surprising, but it is somewhat embarrassing, since any movement so novel and far-reaching is bound to evoke more enthusiasm than discrimination. Thus André Gide, acting on André Malraux's advice, reads William Faulkner and Dashiell Hammett with equal attention; while an article in *Les temps modernes,* after deploring the taste of French translators, dismisses Katherine Anne Porter and Kathleen Winsor in the same breath.[1] European criticism has sometimes recognized the qualities of neglected American genius: for example, the English recognition of Melville. Yet often, as in the Russian cult of Jack London, a writer has been extravagantly praised for qualities which are not especially striking to other

Americans. When the Russians admire Howard Fast, or the Germans exalt Thomas Wolfe, their reasons are not far to seek. The same play, Thornton Wilder's *Skin of Our Teeth,* is welcomed in Catholic Bavaria for its rediscovery of original sin and condemned in Marxist Russia for its cyclical theory of history.[2]

When Jean-Paul Sartre visited this country a few years ago, he clarified for readers of the *Atlantic Monthly* why his approach to American literature differed so very candidly from theirs.[3] Why, he asked, read Henry James when Flaubert is accessible? European readers, weary of time, seeking perennial youth with André Gide, turn from the traditional to the contemporary. Local color, the Wild West, highways and byways of the Jack London territory, make a stronger impression on them than upon ourselves. My colleague, F. O. Matthiessen, reported that Czechoslovakian students see through *The Moon Is Down,* yet fail to notice the defects of *Cannery Row.*[4] In other words, they know that John Steinbeck romances when he writes about Norwegians, yet they eagerly swallow his romantic Californians. Although they may confound myths with documents, their real concern is with subject rather than style. As for their neighbors, the Swedes, when they awarded the Nobel Prize to Pearl S. Buck in 1938, they gratified a naive documentary interest in still remoter areas of the world. Our two compatriots who preceded her, Sinclair Lewis and Eugene O'Neill, had almost been professionally American. "Books are not written to last in America," says Denis de Rougemont, a Swiss who has taken up American journalism, "but to strike and agitate as quickly and as fully as possible."[5]

The figure of the American man of letters that emerges to sweep his European admirers off their feet is a reporter, a soldier, a sportsman, anything but a literary man. Par excellence he is Ernest Hemingway, and lets nothing intervene between actions, emotions, and the surface of his prose. Those who feel overburdened with the past, overconscious of artifice, cultivate in him—as Emilio Cecchi points out—"the illusion of having finally hit upon a literature which has nothing to do with literature, which is not spoiled or weakened by literature."[6] But Signor

Cecchi, who is too well read to be taken in by that illusion, goes on to acknowledge Faulkner's literary debts to Anderson, Joyce, Conrad, and Flaubert. Conversely Mario Praz finds, in younger Italian writers like Elio Vittorini and Giuseppe Berto, an indebtedness to the proletarianizing influence of transatlantic fiction.[7] The resulting synthesis may be what philosophers discern at the end of a historical cycle: an interfusion of decadent culture with barbarian energy. But there are at least as many interpretations as there are countries, and we can only take soundings here and there. Though we must not look for one consistent and comprehensive view, we may profitably ask what significant attitudes are manifested in England, France, and Russia.

First let us look toward England, where we stand in a special relationship—that relation between colony and mother country which latter-day history has all but reversed. The strongest continuity, which of course is our language, can be traced through successive editions of H. L. Mencken's rich compilation; the American language, having gradually attained its autonomy, has more recently asserted a counterinfluence over English speech. Similar trends are reported from the book market. Books that were sold on a scale of 100,000 copies or more, during the 1920s and 1930s in England, seem to have all been of American authorship.[8] The unanticipated British success of *Babbitt*, which started the trend, gave Sinclair Lewis the opportunity to unfurl a declaration of independence. But the literary revolution had already been fought and won when the copyright issue was settled, when Oxford presented its doctorate to Mark Twain, when England's foremost novelist was Henry James. Dean Inge was now ready to acknowledge the cultural dependence of the mother country. "The Americans are our masters," he announced; and though the prospect held little to cheer his native pessimism, it ironically answered the question raised by Sydney Smith a century before: "In the four quarters of the globe who reads an American book?"[9]

But ironies work both ways, and in this instance the way was open for English writers in the United States, just as the Scots had sought their fortunes in eighteenth-century London. The visiting Englishman, with his certain condescension, is hardly a stranger to the American scene. Such transient Georgian relics as the Sitwells, however, are rare today. An Evelyn Waugh may return to England declaring that the good life is impossible in America; yet thereupon, declaring that Americans talk too much, he recrosses the Atlantic for another lecture tour. More common is the British novelist in residence, who oscillates between Hollywood and theosophy, thereby enjoying the worst of both worlds, like Aldous Huxley or Christopher Isherwood. When Huxley and Waugh satirize the American way of life, it somehow resists their satire—not because it is invulnerable but because it is fairly tough, while their techniques are too brittle, their values too sentimental. The turmoil that made our continent a haven for English-speaking culture has also enriched it with exiles from the European continent. The wave of the thirties swept home, with what they had picked up abroad, our expatriates of the twenties. The Americanization of W. H. Auden recharted the traditional direction that T. S. Eliot's British passport had pointed.

The effect of these migrations has not been, in any organized sense, to make this hemisphere the literary center; rather it has functioned as an agent for the decentralization and diffusion of European literature. When Auden arrived, he propounded the paradox that American gregariousness isolated the poet and left him to the lonely rigors of artistic creation. Cyril Connolly carries this paradox to the point of *non sequitur*: "The peculiar horrors of America—its brashness, music at meals, and racial hysteria— . . . force the onlooker into a rejection of the world . . ."[10] Rejection perhaps, but more probably acceptance, or some farfetched compromise between the yogi and the scenario writer. Connolly compares his own arrival, and Auden's greeting, to the encounter between the country-mouse and the city-mouse in Disney's film. Connolly's subsequent grand tour of America, undertaken on behalf of his magazine *Horizon,* seems to have comprehended nothing between the intellectual circles of New York City and the artists' colonies of California, between Auden and Henry Miller—the latter sheltered by "a romantic shack" from such peculiar horrors as fastidiousness would instinctively reject. Connolly is not an outgoing onlooker. When he mentions a widely circulated and highly extroverted book about a chicken farm, whether by Freudian lapse or typographical error, he calls it *The Ego and I.*

During the preceding year Mr. Connolly had been nettled by an American review, which—I regret to say—I happened to write. I only allude to it now because of his editorial retort, which—modestly if not quite candidly—concealed the fact that a book of his was the object of my criticism and conveyed the impression that I had attacked the corpus of contemporary British writing. Our cross-grained and cross-purposed repartee is somewhat less than the stuff of an international incident, and Mr. Connolly is no more willing than I to be bullied into assuming a chauvinistic position. But what should interest others is his willingness to go much farther than I in conceding the superiority of particular American writers, even suggesting genetic or psycho-sexual reasons for British inferiority. "Well, there are three writers I envy America," he writes, "Hemingway as a novelist, Edmund Wilson as a critic, and E. E. Cummings as a poet. America possesses many more good writers, but those three have something which we are inclined to lack (perhaps because they are father's boys and our literature is apt to be made by those more influenced by their mothers) : that is to say, they are illusion-free and unite a courageous heart-whole emotional drive to an adult and lively intellectual toughness."[11] Later he sums up the distinction, as other British critics have done, in terms of comparative virility: *"Our impotence liberates their potentialities."*

To such opinions a vigorous dissent must be registered in the name of George Orwell. As a specialist in popular culture, Orwell does not feel the esthete's need to stand in awe before the semi-literate or the antiliterary; indeed he is not hesitant to play the moralist when he feels called upon. He agrees that the cultural impetus has been shifting to America, but he thoroughly deplores the shift; not the hypercivilized Old World, but the barbaric

New, is for him the breeding place of decadence. He contrasts the old-fashioned boys' weeklies—which, for all their old-school-tie snobbishness, professed a code, a notion of "cricket," an ideal of "playing the game"—with the so-called "Yank mags" that invaded England during the war, "written in a jargon that has been perfected by people who brood endlessly on violence."[12] As opposed to the schoolboy idealism of Raffles, the gentleman crook, Orwell instances a current shocker, *No Orchids for Miss Blandish.* Here, under the influence of a Chicago setting and a Faulkner theme, an English novelist has gone beyond mere materialism to "realism" in its Machiavellian implications—in other words, a fascist lust for power. The critics we next consider, the Russians, consider our writers fascists because they are not realistic enough.

With England our problems are those of emphasis and adjustment, within the framework of shifting but more or less familiar conditions. With Russia we have more fundamental grounds for cleavage—cultural and linguistic divergences as wide as our two nations and the civilization that falls between them, ideological differences which can be theoretically transcended but interpose practical obstacles every day. The key to the literary misunderstandings between the Russians and ourselves may be found in that ambiguous term *realism.* Though we pride ourselves on being "realistic"—that is to say, hard-boiled—our traditional fiction is didactic, allegorical, romantic. Our naturalistic school was a late development, largely a conscious importation from Europe, notably from France. Somewhat the same tradition of social protest and self-criticism developed, despite the czars, in nineteenth-century Russia. When the Soviets took over, and the opposition became an orthodoxy, "socialist realism" became the party line. Marxist criticism perforce supported the authoritarian regime, though it remained severely critical of life and literature in other countries. Meanwhile, in democratic countries, realists freely continue to criticize life as they find it, thus supplying a dialectical antithesis which very neatly fits the Marxian thesis.

The Russians admit no inconsistency in the fact that their realism, which once protested, now glorifies. Not the literary method but the social situation, they maintain, has been changed by revolution into its opposite. They would point to the pivotal example of Gorki as the realist who weathered the change. Even his prerevolutionary drama, *The Lower Depths*, contains a note of affirmation: "The word *man* sounds proud!" Whereas, for the vagrants depicted by Eugene O'Neill in *The Iceman Cometh*, a Soviet critic declares that the word *man* sounds "low and rotten."[13] For the Russians it is not socialist realism but bourgeois realism which has fallen away. In 1946 it was estimated that some forty million copies of American books had been published in Russia since 1917. Among them the strongly marked preference has been for writers who flourished during the muckraking years of the early twentieth century—most appropriately for Theodore Dreiser. The extraordinary vogue of Upton Sinclair, which began when Tolstoy recommended *The Jungle* to the Russian public, has reached the stage where a current magazine calls him "the most important writer in contemporary America."[14] Lanny Budd to the contrary notwithstanding, the same article insists that plutocracy is forcing Sinclair to publish his own books, and presents an account of American publishing practices which is largely derived from *The Brass Check* (1919).

Such American qualities as the Russians admire come to a dead end, it would seem, in the books of our immediate contemporaries. In the Soviet Union, as in the United States, the writer tends to be an unliterary man; the novelist is becoming a superior journalist; and the most esteemed book is the plain, unvarnished tale. But, unlike most of the Western Europeans, the Russians believe that our recent writing has been sicklied over with what they call *literaturshchina*, "literariness." Faulkner and Henry Miller reveal to them a kind of "witches' sabbath," which celebrates the decadence of our culture as well as the decay of our society. Even the popularity of Steinbeck and Erskine Caldwell, who were welcome and sympathetic visitors to Russia a few years ago, has recently been attacked in a public lecture. The lecturer, M. Mendelson, accused Caldwell of creating "monotonous biologically conditioned monstrosities" and Steinbeck of "insistently emphasizing the biological undertones."[15] Such criticisms are quite understandable; it is harder to understand why a Communist critic, who presumably believes in scientific materialism, should use the language of science so pejoratively. However, the subject of biology, along with various intellectual questions, is currently under revision in the U.S.S.R.

The Marxists are more consistent when they attack "the renegadism of liberal intelligentsia," the backsliding of American fellow travelers, the rediscovery of so-called spiritual values by Lewis Mumford and Van Wyck Brooks.[16] Professional philistines like J. Donald Adams are approvingly cited in the Soviet press whenever they disapprovingly refer to the pessimism of our more serious novelists. As for our poets, their pens are weapons enlisted in the service of reaction, seeking to "disarm people for the war against fascism and to spread cynicism, defeatism, and other fascist ideas."[17] E. E. Cummings is compared to Goebbels, while the poems of Robinson Jeffers belong to "the fifth column of literature." Fortunately—or unfortunately—there seem to be certain exceptions, but to name them here would be to do them a disservice; for their poetic virtues are measured solely by an ideology which would seem progressive to the Cominform and subversive to a congressional committee. Failure to adhere to party lines is as damaging in one moral climate as straight adherence is in the other—if adherence, in these days of sudden twists and sinuous turnings, can indeed be straight. At the moment the odds are large that any American writer, judged by the canons of Soviet criticism, will be indicted as a lackey of capitalistic imperialism.

Can one culture ever have shown toward another, at the very same time, such eager attention and such uniform disapproval? Can it be that the Russians protest too much, or are we simply unused to the harsh accusations of Marxist controversy? After all, they have dealt no less harshly with many of their own leading artists, and they seem to regard the word *putrid* as the hall-mark of critical acumen. When Ilya Ehrenburg denounces Western intellectuals as "idiots" and "dolts," he may be merely dodging the suspicion of cosmopolitan urbanity that some of his compatriots hold against him. At all events, unreasoning hostility seems to be part of a Russian counteroffensive, planned with an eye upon the friendlier reception that American writers are getting in Western Europe. "Along with the shopworn goods that are disposed of by the Marshall Plan," writes the Soviet critic, Ivan Anisimov, "America trades widely in its literature. Slavish criticism in France, as in other occupied countries, obsequiously praises the 'gifts' of American literature. These cheaply bought delights cannot conceal the fact that, under the guise of literature, America exports wastage, rottenness, lies."[18] It confirms our lack of communication with Russia, as well as our present closeness to the French, that the latter should look for truth in this doubtful cargo.

For, without a doubt, the conclusion of the war brought with it "a Franco-American cultural offensive," launched in the United States and profusely greeted in France. Though the currents of transatlantic influence now run eastward rather than westward, the two cultures still preserve their peculiar traits; it is simply that France, for so long the exporter of elegance, has begun to import a kind of American toughness. A French professor at Princeton University, Maurice-Edgar Coindreau, by his translations of Faulkner and other contemporaries, has decisively contributed to this movement. The publishing list of the *Nouvelle revue française*, in its *Série noire*, carries each month the scarifying titles of California thrillers, *traduits de l'américain*. One of the most enterprising translators, Marcel Duhamel, after a performance of his version of *Tobacco Road*, was asked why he translated so many plays "from the American." He replied that he did so because it was easier than to translate plays from the French.[19] Despite their zeal for immediacy and sensationalism, the importers have not neglected our older writers: witness the translation of *Moby Dick* by Jean Giono and others, or such critical studies of Melville as Jean Simon's. Yet a recent French visitor, meditating for a moment at Concord, discerns the world of Damon Runyon in the village of Emerson.[20]

It is we who are undiscriminating, not they, the French admirers of our literature argue. They appreciated Henry Miller before we did—before we do. We are too simple; he is too ambiguous for us, according to Maurice Blanchot.[21] If we make the mistake of thinking him unambiguous, we read him single-mindedly and therefore low-mindedly; he is never really obscene, he is merely fantastic. Apology yields to eulogy in the preface to the French translation of *Tropic of Cancer,* where we are told that Miller is as subtle as Proust, as vigorous as Joyce, as comprehensive as Balzac, and as brutal as Shakespeare.[22] Choice of phrase and clarity of thought, those virtues for which we traditionally admire French criticism, fade and blur before the American onrush. Miller's expatriate Bohemianism, for another critic, fuses together the cosmic and the nostalgic: "Brooklyn calls Montparnasse, Montparnasse Brooklyn; Cancer answers Capricorn; the Pont de Sèvres evokes all the bridges in the world . . ."[23] T. S. Eliot, at the other extreme, is beginning to draw upon his laureled head the scorn that stigmatizes an academic elder. He is more of an English gentleman than an American poet, says Jean de Boschère, who goes on to accuse the Nobel Prize committee of betraying their obligations to poetry.[24]

American writers on their native ground have again become a subject for observation by traveling French writers. Simone de Beauvoir notes, in her sharp-eyed travel book, *L'Amérique au jour le jour,* that "America is hard on intellectuals." It is instructive to match her impressions of the New York intelligentsia against Mary McCarthy's article, "America the Beautiful," where one such encounter is seen from the other side.[25] Mlle. de Beauvoir was armed for something more positive; Miss McCarthy feels embarrassed at being so negative. If I may hark back to Connolly's fable, the roles of the country-mouse and the city-mouse are reversed. The absence of solidarity in American liter-

ary life seems particularly striking to Mlle. de Beauvoir's fellow
Existentialist, Jean-Paul Sartre, who has been so active in Parisian
coteries and artistic schools. The plight of the artist, isolated
from society, yet engaged in a struggle for its freedom and his
own, is typified for Sartre by Richard Wright. As a Negro, Wright
cannot do otherwise; he cannot disengage himself, like Flaubert,
to practice belles-lettres. What Europe means to Sartre on the
plane of time, America means on the plane of space; Americans
are "men on the loose, lost in a continent too big for them, as we
have lost ourselves in history."[26]

Sartre explains the widespread French imitation of modern
American fiction as "the defense mechanism of a literature which,
feeling threatened because its techniques and myths were no
longer enabling it to face the historical situation, grafted foreign
methods upon itself, so that it could fulfil its function by new
experiments." Thus in his novel, *Le sursis,* Sartre adapted a
technique from Dos Passos—who had adapted it in turn from
Joyce—for presenting the theme of disorder within an ordered
structure. And in his play, *La putain respectueuse,* he created a
myth from the facts of the Scottsboro case, which not only
dramatized an American dilemma, but stated the moral problem
that Frenchmen faced during the years of collaboration and resistance. The word *south,* so rich in its European connotations,
as Mlle. de Beauvoir points out, connotes the most tragic part
of America, "the land of slavery and hunger."[27] With its racial
tension, its meaningless violence, its personal alienation, it could
just as well be North Africa, as Albert Camus suggests in
L'étranger. And if, as Camus elsewhere suggests, the human condition is that of Sisyphus, going through his motions eternally
and ineffectually, it is easy to understand French admiration for
a novel about an American dance marathon: Horace McCoy's
They Shoot Horses, Don't They?

Anxiety within, absurdity without, the existential outlook, the
effort to control himself where man has lost control over his
circumstances—is there anything in such a situation that confines it to one hemisphere or the other? "What gives American

literature the glamor it has for us today is not that it is more talented than ours," declares Maurice Nadeau, "but that it expresses more forcefully, more sincerely, and more brutally the despair of our time."[28] Such considerations, matters not of kind but of degree, differentiate Sartre from Dos Passos, Céline from Miller, or Malraux from Hemingway. The New World speaks with characteristic liveliness; but it speaks of troubles that beset the Old World; and to this extent our writers, at the midpoint of the twentieth century, have gone back upon the well-known optimism of their forerunners. Shortly after World War I, André Gide set down in his journal this sentence from Walther Rathenau: "America has no soul and will not deserve to have one until it consents to plunge into the abyss of human sin and suffering."[29] At the end of the last war, Gide told an imaginary reporter that America had abandoned its soulless contentment, its trust in material progress, and had taken the plunge.

We have sampled a small but, I believe, representative portion of the accumulating testimony. Within the three areas that have particularly concerned us, individual views have run closely parallel; but each of the three, collectively considered, registers a different attitude. Our literature is shared by England, repulsed by Russia, embraced by France. The only response that seems common to all is an inclination to see their problems reflected in our mirrors. The British lecturer finds new opportunities for satirizing Anglo-Saxon mores; the Russian Marxist pounces on further deviations from the party line; the French Existentialist is obsessed with the conditions of his own existence. Yet sometimes, when the angle of determination is known, the most oblique refraction can be the most revealing. We have much to learn from the exaggerations of our critics. The British remind us that our sudden international ascendancy is—more than a simple matter of bombs and loans—a cultural responsibility. The Russians can teach us something about ideology, that mysterious allegiance which unites some men while dividing others, which sets up barbed-wire entanglements between nations as well as

classes. The French, enlarging our critical perspective, can lend
a moral and universal scope to the social and regional issues confronting our writers.

Lest we confine ourselves to mere opinion—or, what is slighter,
to my generalizations about the opinions of others—let me cite
one startlingly concrete example. American novels are not merely imitated in Europe today, they are fabricated; and one of
these synthetic products—perhaps by an oversight on the part
of our customs authorities—is available for examination. Its very
title is a commentary: *J'irai cracher sur vos tombes*. Its professed translator, Boris Vian, who writes for *Les temps modernes*
under the candid pseudonym of *Le Menteur*, appears to be its
actual author. Its apocryphal author is one Vernon Sullivan, a
Negro whose books are said to be unpublishable in the original
American, but who has undergone the translucent influence of
Faulkner, Miller, and especially James M. Cain. His story is a
nightmarish fulfillment of the recurrent southern fantasy that
every colored man aspires to rape the white man's daughters
and sisters. The hero, who is also the narrator, has Scandinavian
as well as Negro blood. His ambiguous blondness allows him to
pass among the whites, where he sadistically revenges the lynch-
ing of a younger brother. His racial vendetta drives him across
the limbo that separates existentialism from pornography, and
leads him to be masochistically lynched in the end.

The book is not in its own words, *une réunion de l'école du
Dimanche*. To our language, our fiction, our jazz, M. Vian is
nothing if not hep. His local color is vague, however; for though
a reference to *le sénateur Balbo* presumably locates the scene in
Mississippi, the village rather untypically contains a bookshop,
which is opened and shut by a typical Parisian *rideau de fer*.
The bookseller offers a literary formula: "It's easy to be audacious in this country; you have only to say what anyone who
takes the trouble can see."[30] The assumption is that our most
sensational novels are direct transcriptions from American life—
an assumption disproved by the paradox of the book itself, which
is based not on firsthand experience but sheer book knowledge.

Yet if an indigenous school of writing can be so grotesquely parodied by a foreigner, it must show certain pervasive tendencies; if its twisted characters and brutal incidents are not social documents, they must at any rate be psychological myths. The Negro is its dramatic protagonist because he is our displaced person; the conflict it dramatizes is what Gunnar Myrdal has termed our dilemma. Our tragic region is the South, even as our epic theme is the Civil War. Hence any resemblances between our history and postwar Europe are more than coincidental.

The European success of *Gone with the Wind* has significantly coincided with a decade of invasion, occupation, displacement, dispossession, and reconstruction. The lost cause that appealed so strongly to readers in occupied countries, the implied analogy between the Yankees and the Nazis, are signs that life occasionally does better than literature. *Uncle Tom's Cabin,* sweeping across the Continent, was a happier omen, since it presaged liberation for the slaves; whereas Margaret Mitchell's *roman-fleuve* cultivates the unreconstructed nostalgia of the masters. More vital questions are raised by the Continental reception of Steinbeck's *The Grapes of Wrath.*[31] Its translation was officially sponsored, in Nazi Germany and Fascist Italy, because its painful depiction of the underdog's plight was expected to make for anti-American propaganda. The expectation backfired in both countries, partly because of the disparity in standards of living. What most impressed Germans and Italians was that the Okies, however humble their lot, had their jalopies. To thoughtful readers it occurred that a civilization which allowed its writers to attack its defects possessed, at least, the redeeming virtue of self-criticism. To those of little faith, who loudly fear that we expose ourselves too vulnerably when we permit the exposures of our realists to circulate, that result should underline the distinction between critical and totalitarian realism.

"There is an American anguish in the face of Americanism," Jean-Paul Sartre has written. "There is an ambivalence of anguish which simultaneously asks 'Am I American enough?' and 'How can I escape from Americanism?' "[32] If anything can redeem us, it is this hesitation between our optimists and our pessimists, our frontiersmen and our expatriates. Once we rush to the one extreme or the other, we are lost. On the one hand we have a unique background, which would be quite barren if it remained unique. On the other hand we are strengthened by a hybrid strain, the cross-fertilization of many different cultures. What is commonly regarded as peculiarly American is blatant and standardized: Ford, Luce, Metro-Goldwyn-Mayer. What is most original is most traditional: Melville. Moving, in T. S. Eliot's phrase, "Between two worlds become much like each other," these opposites are neutralized.[33] As André Siegfried predicted, Europe is Americanized and America is Europeanized.[34] Organization reconquers the Old World, chaos is rediscovered in the New. Beyond the clamor, beneath the surfaces of the present, the past continues, and our brightest lights are those that keep burning underground. So a young English poet, John Heath-Stubbs, in a sonnet on Hart Crane, invokes America:

> . . . a hollow land,
> Where with false rhetoric through the hard sky
> The bridges leap, twanged by dry-throated wind,
> And crowded thick below, with idiot eye,
> The leaning deadmen strive to pierce the dim
> Tunnels and vaults, which agate lamps illume.[35]

Notes

[1] Boris Vian, "Chronique du Menteur," *Les temps modernes,* vol. 11–12, p. 362 (August–September 1946).

[2] Hanns Braun, "Das Mysterium Iniquitatis bei Thornton Wilder," *Hochland,* vol. 39, no. 5 (June 1947), p. 473.

[3] Jean-Paul Sartre, "American Novelists in French Eyes," *Atlantic Monthly,* vol. 178, no. 2 (August 1946), pp. 114–18.

[4] F. O. Matthiessen, *From the Heart of Europe* (New York: Oxford, 1948) 24.

[5] Denis de Rougemont, "Rhétorique américaine," *Fontaine,* vol. 27–28, p. 14 (June–July 1943).

[6] Emilio Cecchi, "Introduzione," *Americana: Raccolta di Narratori,* ed. Elio Vittorini (Milan: Bompiani, 1943) xvi.

[7] Mario Praz, "Hemingway in Italy," *Partisan Review,* vol. 15, no. 10 (October 1948), pp. 1086–1100.

[8] Malcolm Cowley, "American Books Abroad," *Literary History of the United States* (New York: Macmillan, 1948) II, 1378.

[9] W. T. Spoerri, *The Old World and the New: A Synopsis of Current European Views on American Civilization* (Zurich: M. Niehan, 1937) 73.

[10] Cyril Connolly, "Introduction," *Horizon*, vol. 93–94, p. 11 (October 1947).

[11] Harry Levin, "Self-Condemned Playboy," *New Republic*, vol. 115, no. 2 (July 15, 1946), p. 49; Cyril Connolly, "Comment," *Horizon*, vol. 80, p. 70 (August 1946).

[12] George Orwell, *Dickens, Dali, and Others* (New York: Reynal, 1946) 101.

[13] Vladimir Rubin, "Krisis sovremennoi amerikanskoi literatury," *Zvezda*, August 1948, p. 201.

[14] Ivan Anisimov, "Literatura na sluzhbe reaktzii," *Oktyabr*, October 1948, pp. 176, 183.

[15] M. Mendelson, *Sovremennaya amerikanskaya literatura* (Moscow, 1947) 17, 19.

[16] A. Startzev, "Imperialisticheskaya agressiya i sovremennaya amerikanskaya literatura," *Znamya*, November 1948, p. 128.

[17] Rubin in *Zvezda*, 197.

[18] Anisimov in *Oktyabr*, 179.

[19] Vian in *Les temps modernes*, vol. 21, p. 177 (June 1947).

[20] Simone de Beauvoir, *L'Amérique au jour le jour* (Paris: P. Morihien, 1948) 290.

[21] Maurice Blanchot, "De Lautréamont à Miller," *L'arche*, vol. 3, no. 16 (June 1946), p. 137.

[22] Henri Fluchère, "Le lyrisme de Henry Miller," *Cahiers du Sud*, vol. 32, no. 273 (2nd semester 1945), p. 668.

[23] Jean Quéval, "Henry Miller," *Poésie 47*, vol. 37, p. 110 (January–February).

[24] Jean de Boschère, "T. S. Eliot vu par un témoin," *L'age nouveau*, vol. 33, p. 18 (January 1949).

[25] Beauvoir, *L'Amérique*, 47; Mary McCarthy, "America the Beautiful," *New Directions 10* (New York, 1948) 23–25.

[26] Sartre, *Situations, II* (Paris: Gallimard, 1948) 202, 255, 256.

[27] Beauvoir, *L'Amérique*, 86.

[28] Maurice Nadeau, "Que pensez-vous de la littérature américaine?" *La revue internationale*, vol. 3, no. 13 (February 1947), p. 115.

[29] André Gide, *Imaginary Interviews*, tr. Malcolm Cowley (New York: Knopf, 1944) 146.

[30] Boris Vian, *J'irai cracher sur vos tombes* (Paris: Editions du Scorpion, 1946) 71, 81, 15.

[31] Sonja Marjasch, *Der Amerikanische Bestseller* (Bern: A. Francke, 1946) 92–95.

[32] Sartre, "Présentation," *Les temps modernes*, vol. 11–12, p. 197 (August–September 1946).

[33] T. S. Eliot, *Four Quartets* (New York: Harcourt, 1943) 35.

[34] Spoerri, *Old World and New*, 70.

[35] John Heath-Stubbs, *The Charity of the Stars* (New York: Sloane, 1949) 66.

Index

Index

Index

151–52. *See also* Christianity, Congregationalism

Renaissance, 16, 19, 47: definition, 4; comparison with present age, 4–5; classical tradition in colonies, 5, 8, 10, 11, 13–14; widespread influence of doctrines, 6–7; concept of Christian gentleman, 6–15; ideal of education, 8–9; concept of civic responsibility, 10–15 *passim*; influence on Richard Lee, 10–11; influence on Robert Carter, 11–13; influence on William Byrd II, 13–14; Jefferson as culmination of Renaissance tradition in America, 14–15; science's contribution to, 154; contemporary poet as preserver of heritage, 166

Representative Men, 109, 118

Reyes, Alfonso, 50

Richards, I. A., 156

Riis, Jacob, 122

Rittenhouse, David, 35

Road Between, The, 129

Romeo and Juliet, 136

Rougemont, Denis de, on American books, 170

Roughing It, 73

Rowlandson, Mary, 52

Rukeyser, Muriel, on Willard Gibbs and science, 160–61

Rush, Benjamin, 35: and social planning, 24–26; on writing in America, 65

Russia, 6, 96, 110: publishing in, 106–7; popularity of American authors in, 117, 169–70; influence of contemporary American literature in, 174–77, 180

Sandburg, Carl, 76

Sandys, George, 5

Sartor Resartus, 80

Sartre, Jean-Paul, 180: on American literature, 170, 179, 182

Scarlet Letter, The, 75, 82, 84

Science, 79: part in education of citizens, 15; declaration of independence of American science, 40; Franklin's contributions to, 40, 41–43; Whitman and evolution, 87–88; effect on vocabulary of poetry, 154–56; effect on realism in

poetry, 157–61; rift between poetry and, 161–66; service to modern poets, 166; limitation for modern world, 165–66

Scott, Sir Walter, 69, 111, 114: Irving and, 49, 53, 57, 58; Hawthorne and, 82

Shakespeare, William, 11, 19, 25, 34, 49, 55, 58, 61, 150, 178: Eliot on, 135, 137; Carlyle on, 149

Sheldon, Rev. Charles Monroe, 115

Shelley, Percy Bysshe, 85, 111, 115

Sidney, Sir Philip, 10, 14

Siegfried, André, 183

Simon, Jean, 178

Sinclair, Upton, 128, 175

Sister Carrie, 121–28 *passim*

Sketch Book, 51, 57, 58, 111, 112

Skin of Our Teeth, 170

Slavery: abolition of, 26; Emerson on, 90, 93; Thoreau on, 97

Smith, Captain John, 5, 17, 21

Smith, Sydney, 120, 171

Social planning, 27: in European heritage, 23–24, 26; Benjamin Rush on, 24–26; Thoreau on, 96–97

"Song of Myself," 67, 88

Spain, 52, 56: influence on Mexico, 50; Prescott and, 48, 51, 53; Irving and, 58, 112; Longfellow and, 58–59, 116; Cooper and, 112–13

Spengler, Oswald, 144, 145

Spirit of the Times, 69

Spy, The, 113

Steinbeck, John, 27, 170: Russian attitude toward, 175–76

Stevens, Wallace, 144, 163: on science, 162; anti-intellectualism of, 165–66

Stowe, Harriet Beecher, 114

Strahan, William, 32, 34, 35

Studs Lonigan, 129

Suave Patria, 50

Sweden, and Pearl Buck, 170

Symbolism, 50, 77, 120

Tate, Allen, 149

Tegnér, Esaias, 53, 61

Theory of Literature, 137, 139

They Shoot Horses, Don't They? 179

Thoreau, Henry David, 49, 56, 57, 79: practical transcendentalism of, 81–82,